AF657384

THE ATLANTIC CRITICAL STUDIES

WILLIAM SHAKESPEARE'S
As You Like It

RATRI RAY

ATLANTIC
PUBLISHERS & DISTRIBUTORS (P) LTD

Published by

ATLANTIC

PUBLISHERS & DISTRIBUTORS (P) LTD

7/22, Ansari Road, Darya Ganj,
New Delhi-110002
Phones : +91-11-23273880, 23275880, 23280451
Fax : +91-11-23285873
Web : www.atlanticbooks.com
E-mail : info@atlanticbooks.com

Branch Office
5, Nallathambi Street, Wallajah Road,
Chennai-600002
Phones : +91-44-64611085, 32413319
E-mail : chennai@atlanticbooks.com

Copyright © Atlantic Publishers and Distributors (P) Ltd., 2008

All rights reserved. No part of this publication may be reproduced, stored in a retrieval system, transmitted or utilized in any form or by any means, electronic, mechanical, photocopying, recording or otherwise, without the prior permission of the copyright owner. Application for such permission should be addressed to the publisher.

Printed in India at Nice Printing Press, A-33/3A, Site-IV, Industrial Area, Sahibabad, Ghaziabad, U.P.

General Preface

The Atlantic Critical Studies are study-aids modelled on the study-aids available in England and America, among other places, and are primarily meant for the students of English Literature of Indian universities.

However, in consideration of the local conditions and the various constraints under which our students have to study—non-availability of relevant critical books, dearth of foreign and Indian journals, inaccessibility to good, well-equipped libraries, just to mention a few of them—the models have been considerably improved upon, both qualitatively and quantitatively.

Thus, while these studies are meant to be comprehensive and self-sufficient, the distinguished scholars who have prepared these study materials, have taken special care to combine lucidity and profundity in their treatment of the texts.

The Select Bibliography at the end is meant not only to acknowledge the sources used but also to help a student in the pursuit of further studies if s/he wants to.

Atlantic Publishers & Distributors (P) Ltd., believe in quality and excellence. These studies will only reconfirm it.

MOHIT K. RAY
Chief Editor [English Literature]
Atlantic Publishers & Distributors (P) Ltd.,
New Delhi

Contents

Contents

Introduction

The Elizabethan age produced an entire galaxy of poets and dramatists and Shakespeare was the brightest star in it. He not only experimented with, but also perfected, all the prevailing modes of contemporary poetry and drama. Be it narrative poetry, sonnets or lyrics, he wrote the best and the same can be said about his plays.

Indeed, no one can equal him in his versatility as a poet. He tried his hand, for example, at every kind of play, writing tragedies, comedies, chronicles and even a farce. This cannot be said about every dramatist of his time. Marlowe, for example, write tragedies only and Ben Jonson wrote satirical comedies. These two were the only poets who come near to Shakespeare in the power of their poetic talent. Again, within the different categories of tragedy and comedy there is more variety in Shakespeare than in anyone else. His tragedies cover different countries—England, Scotland, Denmark and Italy so far as space is concerned. When one thinks of the genre, all the four main kinds of tragedies current in Elizabethan times can be found among his works. There is Conqueror tragedy in *Macbeth*, Revenge tragedy in *Hamlet*, the Domestic tragedy in *Romeo and Juliet* and the Villain tragedy in *Othello*. Moreover, such labels, though convenient, fail to convey the impression of richness and complexity that his tragedies give. As far as comedies are concerned, we have Romantic comedies (*Twelfth Night*), Pastoral comedies (*As You Like It*), Problem comedies (*Measure for Measure*), Fairy tales (*A Midsummer Night's Dream*) and Romance like *The Tempest*. When we turn to the History plays, again there is variety, for he wrote about English history as well as Roman history. In each case he took up a popular mode of the time and developed it to such an extent that not only did it bear the stamp of his individual genius but also became a universal play.

This material for his plays comes from many different sources, like contemporary narrative poems, prose romances, old plays, history books, etc. In each case he takes the available material and re-organizes it, rejecting some features, concentrating some, expanding some, till the entire play becomes fully stage-worthy and an immortal work of art. This is but another proof of his sense of organisation.

As You Like It belongs to the group of the Golden Comedies, or Happy, Joyous or Festive Comedies as they are variously called. There are three other comedies within this group, *The Merchant of Venice*, *Much Ado About Nothing*, and *Twelfth Night*. It contains his most charming heroine Rosalind and some of his best-known songs.

There is great variety in his comedies, as has already been pointed out Above. There are, in all, sixteen of them, even without counting *The Merry Wives of Windsor* which scholars agree in calling a farce. These comedies are divided into four distinct phases as follows:

1. The Early Comedies: *The Two Gentlemen of Verona, The Comedy of Errors, Love's Labour's Lost, A Midsummer Night's Dream.*
2. The Golden Comedies: *The Merchant of Venice, Much Ado About Nothing, As You Like It, Twelfth Night.*
3. The Problem Comedies: *Measure for Measure, All's Well that Ends Well, Troilus and Cressida, Timon of Athens.*
4. The Last Romances: *Pericles, Cymbeline, The Winter's Tale, The Tempest.*

It should be remembered that our poet's career began with comedies, because his first play is taken to be *The Two Gentlemen of Verona*. Comparing him with classical comedy-writers Ben Jonson declared:

...when thy socks were on,
Leave thee alone for the comparison
Of all that insolent Greece or haughty Rome
Sent forth, or since did from their ashes come.[1]

REFERENCE

1. Quoted in Brown, John Russell ed., *Much Ado About Nothing* and *As You Like It*: A Casebook, Macmillan, London, 1979, p. 23.

1

The Background

(A) THE SOCIO-POLITICAL BACKGROUND

No individual, or his work can be separated from his background and it is very necessary that the socio-political background of a writer be taken into account when a study of his work is being undertaken. Some of the relevant socio-political events of Shakespeare's time are given below in chronological order, which shall be followed by some more detailed account. Religion was one of the chiefest pre-occupations of the day and consequently the main religious events are mentioned as well as the scientific inventions. Queen Elizabeth's time was one of great geographical expansion as well as military exploits and these too are mentioned below:

A Chronological Table

1558 — Queen Mary I dies. Elizabeth I succeeds.

— Mary Queen of Scots marries the French Dauphin. The French capture Calais.

'59 — Mary Queen of Scots declares herself the Queen of England.

— War between Spain and France ends.

— Church of England re-established more firmly.

'60 — The Scottish Parliament establishes the Reformed Church and breaks with Rome.

'61 — Mary Queen of Scots returns from France. She clashes with the Calvinists.

1562 — The Huguenots begin emigrating from France to England.

'63 — Bubonic plague in Europe.

'64 — *Shakespeare born.* The Anglo-France war ends. England at war with Spain. Galileo born.

— The Thirty-nine Articles adopted by the Church of England. Queen Elizabeth tries to enforce unity of religion.

'67 — Mary Queen of Scots abdicates. Rugby Chapel founded.

'68 — Mary Queen of Scots flees to England. She is held captive by Queen Elizabeth.

'69 — Rebellion of the Roman Catholic earls crushed.

'70 — Pope Pius V excommunicates Queen Elizabeth.

'74 — Burbage gets licence to build the first permanent theatre in London.

'76 — Tycho Brahe begins his astronomical observations. Fifth French Religious war ends.

— Burbage opens the first theatre of England at Shoreditch, in London.

'77 — England makes treaty with the Dutch.

— Sir Francis Drake begins circumnavigation of the globe in the Pelican.

'80 — Sir Francis Drake completes circumnavigation.

'81 — Conversion to Roman Catholicism declared to be a treason in England.

— Galileo discovers the Law of the Pendulum.

'83 — Plot against the Queen.

— Humphrey Gilbert takes possession of Newfound land for England.

'84 — Sir Walter Raleigh discovers names and starts to colonize Virginia.

'86 — England wins the battle of Zutphen in which Sir Philip Sidney gets fatally injured.

1586 — Plot against the Queen. Mary Queen of Scots implicated and convicted of treason.

— Thomas Cavendish begins the third circumnavigation of the globe.

'87 — Rose Theatre built by Henslowe.

— Mary Queen of Scots executed for treason.

'88 — Defeat of the Spanish Armada by Sir Francis Drake.

'89 — Galileo publishes the results of his experiments with falling bodies.

'92 — John Davis discovers the Falkland Islands.

'93 — Absence from the Church on Sundays made punishable by law.

'95 — Southwell the mystical poet is executed for celebrating Mass.

'96 — England, France and Netherlands form an alliance against Spain.

— Peasant revolt in Oxfordshire.

'97 — Second Spanish Armada sent against England is destroyed by a storm.

— Statutory provisions for Poor Relief. Beggary made illegal. Transporting of convicts to colonies.

'98 — The Bodleian Library begun. Globe Theatre opened.

1601 — Earl of Essex raises rebellion against the Queen and is executed.

— The East India Company dispatches its first trading fleet to Sumatra.

'02 — The end of the Irish Rebellion.

— Kepler posits heliocentric theory of the universe.

— Bodleian Library opened.

'03 — Queen Elizabeth dies. Accession of James VI of Scotland as James I of England.

— Plague in England. Amnesty to Irish rebels.

— Sir Walter Releigh sentenced for treason.

1603 — East India Company sends trade mission to India.

'04 — Peace with Spain.

— Banishment of Roman Catholic priests provokes Gunpowder Plot to blow up Parliament Houses.

— Acts against priests and recusants. Anglican canons made.

— Silk manufacture begins in England.

'05 — Gunpowder Plot discovered. Conspirator Guy Fawkes arrested. English colonists land in Barbados.

'07 — First permanent settlement Jamestown is founded on American mainland.

'08 — Failure of plan for union with Scotland.

— Invention of the microscope and telescope in Netherlands.

'10 — Judicial decision against royal proclamations.

— Explorer Hudson sails through Hudson Bay.

'11 — Parliament dissolved.

— Land granted in northern Ireland to Scottish and English Protestants.

'12 — Alliance with German Protestant princes.

— Witches hanged at Lancashire, the last recorded executions for heresy.

— Colonists from Virginia begin setting in Bermuda.

'13 — Princess Elizabeth marries Elector Frederick V.

— Galileo publishes his acceptance of Copernican theory.

'16 — *Shakespeare dies.* Sir Walter Raleigh sets forth in search of El Dorado.

It can be seen how precarious the position of Queen Elizabeth was when Shakespeare was born. Plots against her were being continually hatched at home, and there was continuous warfare with the nations abroad. It took Queen Elizabeth quite a few years to settle firmly on the throne. Mary Queen of Scots was a continual source of trouble and finally when after plotting against the Queen who was, after all, her cousin, she met with the fate proper for a traitor, Queen Elizabeth was more or less secure on the throne. She was a very fine stateswoman and a good sovereign—patriotic as well as courageous. She was tolerant in her religious policies and put an end to religious controversies G.M. Trevelyan points this out:

> In the year in which the Queen succeeded her sister Mary, Puritanism was mainly a foreign doctrine imported from Geneva and Rhineland; when she died it was rootedly and characteristically English.[1]

Her long reign, peaceful and prosperous, helped the spirit of Anglicanism drive deep roots in the country. Again, as the same writer points out:

> At the end of her reign it had become a real religion; its services were dear to many, after more than forty years of use in the ancient churches of England.[2]

Just as there were problems of succession in the beginning of Elizabeth's reign (Mary Queen of Scots being a strong claimant), so were there problems and speculations towards the end of her reign. This was inevitable, as she left no direct or obvious heir to the throne. But during the decades of her reign she gave security and prosperity to her country by her wisdom and moderation.

An important feature of the time was its continuous growth and expansion. The structure of society fostered this spirit. There were class barriers, but these were accepted, not resented. So there were no friction between the classes to hamper any kind of growth. There were the feudal lords and the working classes, but no oppression of the latter by the former. It was the freedom of opportunity for everyone that mattered, not equality. The kind of difference between the lord of the manor and the peasantry that existed in medieval England did not exist in Elizabethan England:

> In Tudor England such rigid lines were rendered impossible by the number and variety of men in intermediate classes and occupations, who were closely connected, in the business and amusement of daily life

> with those above and those below them in social status.... Such was the England known and approved by Shakespeare.[3]

The dignity of labour was no mere theory but a proven fact. Everyone earned a fair wage for work that was done honestly and efficiently. This helped a spirit of self-reliance and self-respect grew in the mind of ordinary people.

Most of the people were responsible self-respecting members of society and as such felt responsible towards the poor and the disabled. So the Poor Law was passed for the relief of the unfortunate. The system of Justices of Peace was instituted in which influential and responsible persons were made to minister justice in minor cases. These Justices of Peace or JPs were, in their turn, controlled by the Privy Council, a higher organization.

By this time the economical side of society also received boost as the factory system was started. This brought about industrial prosperity. Mining improved to such an extent that many metals like lead, copper, iron and tin, which had been scarce, became available in plenty. Coal became cheaper, so homes became warmer. Glass window-panes became available so homes became brighter and lighter.

The great explorer Sir Francis Drake brought national glory by his two important achievements, the circumnavigation of the globe and the defeat of the Spanish Armada. This latter was a landmark achievement for it put an end to threats from the sea. A few years later a second Armada was sent, but it perished in a storm. This acted as national confirmation of the faith that the English were the favoured of God. These were, from every point of view, the days of prosperity, security and also of expansion. G.M. Trevelyan sums up:

> By the end of Elizabeth's reign not only was English commerce and finance thus reviving and expanding on a modern basis, but her ancient rivals were in rapid decline.[4]

This expansion and prosperity continued during the Jacobean Age as well. London continued to grow (it was only one square mile in area when Shakespeare arrived there) and industry flourished. One such example has been given above—silk started being manufactured in England. Not many significant changes took place during the next forty years, for those changes that did take place were political ones, not agricultural or industrial changes. When King James VI of Scotland who was a distant cousin of Queen Elizabeth, acceded to the throne of England as King James I of England, it brought about a union of the royal families of England and Scotland. The two kingdoms remained obstinately separated though the King tried very hard to bring them together. Culturally also, Scotland, though much nearer than Holland, was not so influential as the latter.

In the very first year of his reign King James made peace with Spain, thus removing all obstacles for maritime trade. One the seas were safe, colonization started with great vigour. Settlers from England started moving to the fabled land of New England, Virginia, etc. The seeds of the British Empire were sown even as the Holy Roman Empire was declining. Emigrations were organized by the Virginia Company and the Massachusetts Bay Company. These pioneers were motivated by religious as well as commercial motives. Such events interest the historian. Posterity remembers one name, Shakespeare. According to G.M. Trevelyan:

> His works could never have been produced in any other period than those late Elizabethan and early Jacobean times in which it was his luck to live.[5]

(B) THE LITERARY BACKGROUND

Just as, in Italy, the spirit of the Renaissance manifested itself through painting and sculpture, it found its expression in England through literature. A whole host of gifted poets and dramatists (as well as prose-writers) were living and writing at this time. Shakespeare's work was strongly rooted in fertile soil. A chronological table is given below which takes in the main literary events of the time, the birth and death of prominent literary figures. Some influential works of the continent are also mentioned. It is not possible to include the numerous works that were being written, published and staged during this fruitful time. Only a few shall be mentioned. The table begins with the first performance of *Ralph Roister Doister*, ten years before our poet's birth. Shakespeare's own works are not mentioned as they will be dealt with in the right context (*vide* Ch. 2, *infra*).

A Chronological Table

1554 — Sir Philip Sidney and Lyly born. *Ralph Roister Doister* staged. Bandello's stories published.

'57 — Tottel's *Miscellany*. Cavendish completes the biography of Thomas Wolsey.

'58 — Kyd, Greene, Peele, Lodge born.

'61 — *Gorboduc* performed. Bacon born. Castiglione's *The Courtier*.

'63 — Drayton and Donne born. Foxe's *Book of Martyrs*.

'64 — Shakespeare, Marlowe, Galileo born.

'66 — Gascoigne's *Supposes*. Painter's *Palace of Pleasure*, Vol. I.

'67 — Campion and Nashe born. *Palace of Pleasure*, Vol. II.

'70 — Roger Ascham's *The Schoolmaster*.

'72 — Camoens (Spain) *Os Lusiados*. Donne born.

'73 — Tasso's (Italian) *Aminta*.

'75 — Heywood and Tourneur born.

— *Appius and Viginia,* Gammer Gurton's *Needle*. Fleming's translation of Virgil's Bucolics, Georgics.

'76 — *Paradyse of Daynty Devises*.

'77 — Holinshed's *Chronicles*. Transl. of Ovids *Epistolae Heroidum*

'78 — Lyly's *Euphues*.

'79 — Spenser's *Shepheard's Calendar*. Lord North's transl. of Plutarch's *Lives*. Gosson's *School of Abuse*.

'80 — Montaigne's (French) *Essais*, Bks. I & II.

'82 — Hakluyts' *Voyages*.

'85 — Kyd's *Spanish Tragedy*.

'86 — Sir Philip Sitney dies. Lyly's *Endimion*.

1587 — *Tamburlaine*, Lyly's *Gallathea. The Misfortunes of Arthur*. Monteverdi's (Italian) *Madrigals* Bk I.

'89 — *Jew of Malta* by Marlowe. Puttenham's *Arte of English Poesie.*

'90 — *Faerie Queene,* I-III published. Lodge's *Rosalynde.*

'91 — Sidney's *Astrophel and Stella*, Peele's *Old Wives' Tale*, Marlowe's *Edward II.*

— Sir John Harington's transl. of Ariosto's *Orlando Furioso* at the Queen's command.

'92 — Revised *Arcadia.* Daniel's *To Delia* (sonnets), Marlowe's *Hero and Leander. Arden of Feversham* (Anon.)

'95 — Spenser's *Amoretti* (Sonnet-sequence), Sidney's *Apology for Poetry.*

'98 — Francis Meres' *Palladis Tamia.*

'99 — Spenser dies. Davies's *Nosce Teipsum.*

1600 — England's *Helicon*, England's *Parnassus*, Jonson's *Cynthia's Revels,* Dekker's Shoemaker's Holiday.

'01 — Dekker and Marston's *Satiromastix*, Jonson's *Poetaster*. Marston's *What You Will.*

'03 — Dowland's *Third Book of Songs*, Heywood's *A Woman Killed with Kindness*, Jonson's *Sejams*, Marston's *The Dutch Courtezan.*

'04 — Chapman's *Bussy D'Ambois*, Marston's *The Malcontent.*

'05 — Drayton's *Collected Poems*, Bacon's *Advancement of Learning*, collaborated play *Eastward Ho*/Middleton's *A Trick to Catch the Old One.*

'06 — Lyly dies, *Yorkshire Tregedy* (Anon.), Jonson's *Volpone*, Tourneur's *The Revenger's Tragedy.*

'07 — Beaumont and Fletcher's *Knight of the Burning Pestle.*

'08 — Fuller and Milton born. Fletcher's *The Faithful Shepherdess*. Chapman's *Duke of Byron.*

'09 — Beaumont and Fletcher's *Philaster*, Fulke Greville's *Mustapha*, Tourneur's *Atheist's Tragedy*.

'10 — Donne's *Pseudo-Martyr*, Jonson's *The Alchemist*.

'11 — Spenser's *Collected Works*, *The Authorised Version of the Bible*. *A King and No King*.

'12 — Crashaw born. Chapman's *Iliad* I-XXIV, Donne's *Second Annivarsarie*, Drayton's *Poly-Olbion*, Webster's *The White Devil*.

'13 — Constable and Overbury die. Purchas's *Pilgrimage*.

'14 — Overbury's *Characters*. Lodge's *Works of Seneca*.

'15 — Sir Walter Raleigh's *History of the World*, Jonson's *Bartholomew Fair*. Webster's *The Duchess of Malfi*.

'16 — Shakespeare dies. Jonson given royal pension. Chapman's *Whole Works of Homer*. Jonson's Works.

As this table shows, the few years from Sidney's birth in 1554 to Shakespeare's death in 1616 cover the best time of literary efflorescence in England. The most familiar names of the Elizabethan and Jacobean times come later than Sidney. The Tudor dynasty had a rose as the emblem and if the literature of the Renaissance is compared with a rose then it can be said that what Sidney saw in his lifetime was only a bud which later opened out to spread out unequalled beauty and fragrance.

Drama, the glory of the Elizabethan and Jacobean era, had barely started in Sidney's time. The plays that were being written and performed were as nothing to those that Shakespeare and others were to write, but it cannot be denied that they prepared the ground for the followers. It is not surprising that Sidney condemned contemporary drama, except for *Gorboduc* which he praised:

> Our tragedies and comedies not without cause cried out against, observing rules neither of honest civility nor of skilful poetry: excepting *Gorboduc* (again I say of those that I have seen) which notwithstanding as it is full of stately speeches and well-sounding phrases, climbing to the height of Seneca's style, and as full of notable

> morality, which it doth most delightfully teach, and so obtain the very end of poesy.[6]

Gorboduc, today, has more of a historical interest than as a work of great literacy merit. Sidney praised it because there was nothing superior to it. *Ralph Roister Doister*, a rollicking comedy, had been staged ten years before Shakespeare's birth. *The Misfortunes of Arthur*, a play in the nature of a history, had been written for the Queen's entertainment in 1587. These works have only historical importance today and cannot by any means be considered seriously as works of great merit.

The prospect is little better than drama when we turn to narrative poetry, songs and sonnets, all of which Shakespeare wrote. Spenser's *Shepheards Calendar* and parts of *Faerie Queene* had been published before Shakespeare's own narrative poems. Tottel had published his famous Miscellany which included the sonnets of Wyatt and Surrey. The famous sequences of Elizabethan love-sonnet started being written by the end of the sixteenth century, reaching their climax in Shakespeare's sequence. The most flourishing genre was that of the lyric. The best lyrics were written by the "Elizabethan nest of singing-birds" from 1580 to 1620, and were being collected and published. Shakespeare's plays are full of songs and, in writing them he took the help of these collections, adapting the words to suit his own requirements. These were mostly light-hearted love-songs:

> The songs-lyric, as developed in accord with the musical art of the time, is too light an instrument to utter the deeper notes of passion and its theme is fanciful love.[7]

As the Elizabethan Age advanced, the output became more and more prolific as well as dazzling. Lyric poetry, narrative poetry, discursive poetry—all flourished in a manner hardly equalled before or since. Prose, which is of minor importance to us (only as the sources of Shakespeare's plays) was developed not only in the romances of Sidney, Lyly and others, but also in the philosophical works of writers like Bacon, Hooker, Sir Thomas Browne *et al.*

It is drama which is the most important of the literacy genres for our present purposes. The University Wits took London by storm by starting with Kyd's *The Spanish Tragedy*, a revenge tragedy in the Senecan mode which was all the rage. This became the archetype for all revenge tragedies. Marlowe's very first attempt *Tamburlaine* (a conqueror tragedy) become so popular that he quickly wrote the second part of the play. As theatres were established, by Burbage and Henslowe, plays were in great demand. The dramatists had ample opportunity for experimenting with different kinds of plays and finding the form that suited them. Shakespeare was specially versatile and no one could rival him in the range of his plays or otherwise, but each of the playwrights could find and settle down with the form that suited him the best, as Ben Jonson did with his humour comedies and Beaumont and Fletcher with their tragicomedies.

The dramatists were highly influenced by classical writers. Seneca for example, was a prevailing influence. Kyd set the example:

> It was the genius of Thomas Kyd that seized upon the essential effects of Senecan action and adapted them, with much relaxation of rules, to the conditions of the public stage.[8]

F.T. Bowers has categorised these tragedies, known as the blood-and-thunder tragedies, into four divisions: Conqueror tragedy (*Tamburlaine*, *Macbeth*, etc.), Revenge tragedy (*The Spanish Tragedy*, *Hamlet*, etc.), Villain tragedy (*The Changeling*, *Othello*, etc.), and Domestic tragedy (*A Women Killed with Kindness*, *Romeo and Juliet*, etc.). There are many tragedies that cannot be contained within just one group. Webster's *The Duchess of Malfi* for example, is a revenge tragedy as well as a domestic tragedy. Shakespeare's *Othello* is a villain tragedy as well as a domestic tragedy.

Comedy too, flourished in the hands of Lyly, Peele, Greene, Shakespeare, Ben Jonson and others. M.C. Bradbrook has divided Elizabethan society into three categories, the Court, the Country and the City, and ascribes different kinds of comedy to each. The comedies of Shakespeare come mostly under the first of these, and those of Ben Jonson under the third. There is great variety within this kind of play. There are Romantic comedies like those written by Shakespeare, Satirical comedies like those of Ben Jonson, Problem comedies like the four written by Shakespeare, tragicomedies like those by Beaumont and Fletcher, and Romances like the last plays of Shakespeare.

Numerous masques were also used for courtly entertainment. Those of Ben Jonson were specially successful. Shakespeare used the device quite frequently in his plays.

Shakespeare's works thus were firmly rooted into the soil of Elizabethan England and he is the ideal product of his milieu. Another poet, four centuries later, points out the relevance of the background:

> No poet, no artist of any art, has his complete meaning alone. His significance, his appreciation is the appreciation of his relation to the dead poets and artists.[9]

REFERENCES

1. Trevelyan, G.M., *Illustrated English Social History*, Vol. 2, Harmondsworth, Penguin Book Ltd., 1964, p. 86.
2. *Ibid.*
3. *Ibid.*, p. 62.
4. *Ibid.*, p. 123.
5. *Ibid.*, p. 125.
6. Enright, D.J. and Chickera, Ernst de, ed., *English Critical Texts: 16th Century to 20th Century,* Oxford, the University Press, 2002, p. 40.
7. Carpenter, Frederick Ives, *English Lyric Poetry: 1500-1700.* London, Blackie & Son Ltd., No. date, p. 47.
8. Craig, Hardin, *The Literature of the English Renaissance: 1485-1660.* New York, Collier Books, 1962, p. 80.
9. Eliot, T.S., *Three Essays*, Calcutta, Oxford University Press, 1979, p. 17.

2

Life and Works

(A) A SHORT BIOGRAPHY

Many biographies of Shakespeare have been written but it cannot be denied that a lot of the details supplied therein are not very dependable. Anecdotes about him abound, but they are more legendary than historical, particularly those about his early life. Details about his later life, specially from the time that his group became accepted at Court, are historically true and fully reliable. As usually happens, in the case of well-known figures, Shakespeare also became invested with an aura of glory, all the more pronounced as this renown was not posthumous but attained during his lifetime. In the seventeenth century Fuller wrote a brief life in his famous *Worthies* (1662) and John Aubrey in his *Lives of Eminent Men*. The first modern editor of Shakespeare, Nicholas Rowe, took material from many other sources as well in the life given in his edition of the plays. More intensive research has been done by modern biographers. It has to be acknowledged however that more material is available on Shakespeare than on his other contemporaries. A chronological table of the important events of his life is given below:

A Chronological Table of the Chief Events of His Life

1564 — Apr. 23, the supposed date of birth of Shakespeare.

— Apr. 26, Shakespeare christened at the local parish church of Stratford-upon-Avon.

'71 — Possible time of enrolment in the local school.

1578 — His father's fortunes undergo reverses and he is, possibly, withdrawn from school at this time, or perhaps later.

'82 — Shakespeare gets married to Anne Hathaway.

'83 — Birth of Susanna, his first child.

'85 — The twins, Hamnet and Judith, are born.

'86 — Shakespeare's supposed departure for London.

'93 — *Venus and Adonis* published by Richard Field.

'94 — *Rape of Lucrece* pub. *Titus Andronicus* staged. *The Taming of the Shrew.*[1]

'95 — *A Midsummer Night's Dream.*

'96 — Death of Hamnet his only son. *Sonnets.*

'97 — Shakespeare buys New Place. *The Merchant of Venice.*

'99 — He buys shares in the Globe Theatre. *Much Ado, As You Like It, Twelfth Night, Henry V, Julius Caesar.*

1602 — The birth of his first grand child. He buys one hundred and seven acres of land. *All's Well that Ends Well, Troilus and Cressida, Hamlet.*

'04 — His company taken under royal patronage and given the name of the King's Men. *Measure for Measure, Othello.*

'05 — *Macbeth.*

'06 — *King Lear.*

'07 — *Timon of Athens.*

'09 — *Coriolanus. Sonnets* published.

'11 — He retires from the company and comes back to his native village. *The Winter's Tale, The Tempest.*

'12 — *Henry VIII.*

'16 — His Last Will and Testament drawn up.

— Apr. 23, Shakespeare dies on his fifty-second birth anniversary.

— Apr. 25, He is buried in the chancel of the Stratford Church.

The exact date of his birth is not known, as the Register of Baptism maintained by the parish church did not record the date of birth but of baptism only. As the official language of the time was Latin, the entry in the Register says:

1564, Apr. 26, Gulielmus Filius Johannes Shakespere.[2]

It was the custom those days to baptize a baby three days after its birth, perhaps because of the prevalence of infant mortality. It is therefore assumed that he was born on the twenty-third of April, in the village of Stratford-upon-Avon, the county being Warwickshire. This was a lucky day for it was St. George's day, England's patron saint.

Not much is known about his childhood days but it can be taken for granted that he spent a happy and secure childhood in the bosom of a loving and prosperous family. His position in the family was a significant one as he was the eldest son. His father John Shakespeare was in the trade and therefore not regarded as a gentleman (i.e., belonging to the class of landed gentry), but was a worthy man in society. Later he was to become the alderman for by this time the little village had expanded enough to have one. This was in 1565 and by this time he was in a position to claim the status of gentleman. Keeping in mind the feudal structure of contemporary society, this fact was of great significance. Socially speaking, Shakespeare's mother came from a family belonging to a higher level, for Mary Arden's father belonged to the class of small landed gentry.

The village was surrounded by a wonderful countryside, and William, as a little boy, would run wild in the lap of benevolent Nature. The memory of this beautiful environment was to produce the lovely and lyrical passages of nature description in his poetry. The sunny glades of the forest of Arden look back to these joyful experiences, though, of course, Shakespeare mentions the freezing skies and the bitter winds of winter as well, for he was not one to shirk the reality.

Another significant fact is that his father was a justice of Peace as well as the high bailiff of Stratford. He had to execute many duties connected with courts of law and Shakespeare, being the eldest son, often accompanied him. He thus gained intimate knowledge of legal procedures, of which the trial scene of *The Merchant of Venice* is the proof.

Queen Elizabeth had established grammar schools all over England in order to educate the commoners. Shakespeare was duly admitted to the local one. He was perhaps seven at this time and did not take kindly to it at all. It is therefore thought that in the passage in *As You Like It* where Jaques refers to the school-boy Shakespeare is referring to himself, or, at least, writing out of personal experience:

> Then the whining school-boy, with his satchel
> And shining morning face, creeping like snail
> Unwillingly to school.[3]

Latin grammar was the most important part of the curriculum in these schools. Boys of the aristocratic class went to exclusive and expensive schools where they got classical education which Shakespeare could not get. But this does not mean that he did not get any education in the classics. Ben Jonson's ridicule of his "small Latin and less Greek" is well-known but most misleading. Shakespeare may not have been a classical scholar of good standard according to contemporary expectations, but he had acquired a fair knowledge of classical literature. Shakespeare was a student here till he was about 14 or 16, it is not known exactly when he left the school.

All these schools in England followed the same curriculum and kept the same hours. School started at six in the morning and went on till five in the evening. There were breaks during the day and there were clear-cut rules which laid down that, in all, there had to be two and a half hours' break spaced out during the day. The curriculum is given below:

Poetry: *The Bucolica* of Mantuan

The Eclogues and *The Aeneid* of Virgil.

The Poems of Horace.

The Metamorphoses of Ovid.

Prose: Caesar, Livy, Cicero.

Drama: Ten tragedies of Seneca.

The comedies of Plautus.

The comedies of Terence.

This makes it quite clear that Shakespeare had a solid foundation of classical education. The classical references that occur continuously in his plays come from first hand knowledge of classical literature. One of his biographers remarks:

> Today all scholars are agreed that Shakespeare was a well-educated man of his times, that he certainly continued to further his education by wide reading throughout his life and that there is no display of learning in any one of his plays which could not have been acquired at the Stratford Grammar School.[4]

There is another opinion that goes totally against this idea of Shakespeare's schooling. It is a well-known fact that the family was a Catholic one and, basing his theory on this fact, John Dover Wilson has argued that John Shakespeare may not have put his son in the Grammar School at all. There were many great Catholic noblemen at the time and he might have sent his son to one such household. Shakespeare might have received his education and gained inside knowledge of the lifestyle of the aristocracy in this manner and depicted it in his plays.

After some years some kind of misfortune had visited the family and John Shakespeare's fortunes went under an eclipse. Shakespeare was taken out of the school in his teens, but it is not known exactly when. It is not known whether he had completed his education by that time either. Every year, every hour of education is of crucial importance at this age, for the mind is more capable of learning at this time than at any other. How much harm it had done to Shakespeare's future career is only to be guessed at.

It was during these highly formative years that Shakespeare first came into contact with stage-performances. Many records exist of different travelling companies of players visiting his village. These itinerant groups were patronized by the great aristocrats of the time and were accordingly named after them. There were groups belonging to the Earls of Leicester, Warwick and Worcester. They staged the traditional moralities as well as the modern five-act plays written in imitation of classical models, like *Gorboduc,* etc.

While still in his teens Shakespeare's sensitive and young mind fell to the charms of the local belle Anne Hathaway from a village that lay at a little distance, named Shottery. She was a much admired and sought after girl, as becomes clear from an anonymous couplet often quoted by his biographers:

> Anne Hathaway, she hath a way
> To charm all hearts, Anne Hathaway.

Young Shakespeare was the one on whom she bestowed her favours and agreed to marry. She was eight years older than him but this was no barrier to the lovers and they got married on November 28, 1582. He was not yet nineteen, whereas she was twenty-six. Next year Susanna their first child, was born. She was baptized on May 26, 1583. Nearly two years later the twins, Hamnet and Judith, were born. Hamnet died in 1596, leaving no one to carry on the line.

Thus, when barely twenty-one, Shakespeare was a man with three children, a wife eight years older than himself and no visible means of earning a livelihood. Nor was his father's financial position at all an enviable one. There are many versions of how he earned a livelihood at this time. John Aubrey, one of the first biographers in English, had recorded that he was teaching in a school near his own village. How far this is true is debatable. Another better-known story is given by a clergyman and the actor Thomas Betterton. This story became so widely known that it is commonly accepted as true, though it is highly debatable how much of truth there is in it. At Charlecote there was a deer park which was the property of one Sir Thomas Lucy. It is said that Shakespeare, along with some other young men, stole a deer from this park. They were all caught and it is said that Sir Thomas had ordered the young men to be whipped and put into prison. It is also said that Shakespeare resented this bitterly and took his revenge on Sir Thomas by portraying him as Justice Shallow the stupid judge in *The Merry Wives of Windsor*, and *Henry IV*. Modern researches, however, have proved that this story is of doubtful authenticity, for Sir Thomas was not the master of Charlecote forest at that time. It has, however, been supposed for a long time that it was this humiliation that acted as a deciding factor behind Shakespeare's leaving Stratford, in 1586, for London.

Another legend connected with this time of Shakespeare's life, is that he had joined one of the itinerant dramatic companies as an actor, spending quite a few years with it. Again, no one is sure of now much of truth there is in this story what had given rise to it is a will left by a rich Lancashire gentleman, leaving a considerable sum to one William Shakeshafte, a player in his service. This name is suggestive, for Shakeshafte is a variant of the surname Shakespeare. Such variants were common in Elizabethan times, for English was as yet a fluid, young language, with its grammar and pronounciation not yet rigidly formulated.

It is known for sure that the dramatic group, the Queen's Men, visited Stratford at this time, and perhaps this made Shakespeare's thoughts turn towards London. Many other groups also came there and Shakespeare had become familiar with theatrical productions while still young. In 1583, for example, three well-known groups produced plays at Stratford. Two famous and well-organised groups had come there in 1587. Many of his biographers think that he had acted in these. Hamlet's well-known conversation with the players gives evidence of first hand knowledge not only of acting but of stagecraft as well.

The period stretching from 1586 to 1592 is known as the Dark Years, for little is known of them. As record of facts are non-existent, anecdotes exist in great profusion. It is said that he would be loitering outside the playhouses in order to earn a little money by looking after the horses of the gentlemen who came riding to watch the plays. Another legend has it that he was a prompter's assistant. What is known for sure is that he had found a fellow villager named Richard Field who had left Stratford before Shakespeare did and had become an established printer by this time. This friend published his *Venus and Adonis* in 1593 and *The Rape of Lucrece* the next year, both of which became instantly popular. His literary career thus, had begun with narrative poems which were very popular at this time.

In the field of drama, his only serious rival at this time was Marlowe, and it is a remarkable coincidence that the two of them, each independently had reached London at the same time. The two Chronological Tables given above show that they had been born the same year also. This decade (the eighties) was a highly prosperous and stimulating one. Sir Francis Drake was scouring the Spanish Main and Sir Philip Sidney was in the process of writing the first sequence love-sonnets, *Astrophel and Stella*. Perhaps his monumental prose romance *Arcadia*, also, was being drafted at the same time. Out in Ireland, Spenser was composing his poetical masterpiece, *The Faerie Queene*. One by one the members of the group of learned young men, the University Wits, were converging towards London. Lyly, the leader of the group, had already produced his *Euphues* and was now turning towards drama. Two of his romantic comedies, *Campaspe* and *Sappho and Phaon* were performed for the Queen by the choir of the Chapel Royal in 1584. It was *Euphues*, that brought him fame. It was so popular with the ladies that Lyly had declared the hope that:

> Euphues had rather lie shut in a lady's casket than open on a scholar's study.[5]

London, in other words was the centre of cultural and other activities. Marlowe's *Tamburlaine* was presented in 1587, and by then Shakespeare was definitely present there. It was a truly wonderful time of expansion and therefore of enthusiasm, with horizons receding farther and farther in every field. This was the London to which Shakespeare came. F.E. Halliday remarks:

> Shakespeare had arrived in London at the most thrilling moment in its history; thrilling, however not only because of danger, anxiety, expectation and hope in the air, but also because the long-awaited dramatic revival was now imminent.[6]

Shakespeare watched and avidly learned from, the play that were being staged, perhaps acting minor parts in them. He must have been consolidating his position in literary London slowly but surely because his works had become important enough to be noticed by such a well established University Wit as Greene. It is he who is always cited as being the first contemporary to have mentioned Shakespeare's name. It occurs in a pamphlet remembered today chiefly for this reason, named *Greene's Groats-worth of Wit bought with a Million of Repentance*. At the end of this there is a letter addressed to Peele, Nashe and, of course, Marlowe. He warns them against actors, particularly against a certain actor, in a highly allusive manner. There can be no doubt that the reference is to Shakespeare whom he ridicules and castigates in offensive terms:

> Yes, trust them not: for there is an upstart crow, beautified with our feathers that with his Tyger's heart wrapt in a Player's hyde, supposes he is as well able to bombast out a blank verse as the best of you: and being an absolute Johannes Factotum, is in his own conceit the only shake-scene in a country.[7]

Two clear clues indicate our poet in this famous sentence. The line "Tyger's heart wrapt in a player's hyde" is a deliberate misquotation of Shakespeare's line "O tiger's heart wrapped in a woman's hide" in *Henry VI, PT. III*. Next there is the word "shake-scene" which is a sarcastic reference to our poet's name. This kind of reference speaks volumes about Greene's spitefulness and jealousy, but also makes it clear that by this time Shakespeare had become important enough to cause alarm to the reigning dramatists. This reference occurred in 1592 and from now onwards there are frequent bits of information on him. To have made a mark in six years is no mean achievement for the ignorant country yokel as he must have appeared to the sophisticated and well-established University Wits.

At this time he was still learning his craft and these years are known as the years of apprenticeship. He was, however, not merely learning, but producing also. The sonnet-sequence to Mr. W.H., the two narrative poems, the *Henry VI* trilogy, *Richard III, Titus Andronicus, The Comedy of Errors. The Two Gentlemen of Verona* and *The Taming of the Shrew* were all churned out at this time. They were all highly successful. It seems surprising today that an unsubtle blood-and-thunder tragedy like *Titus Andronicus* was so popular in its day that it was published in 1594 and the title-page reveals its success:

> ...as it was played by the Rt Hon. the Earl of Derby, the Earl of Pembroke and the Earl of Sussex their servants.[8]

These three were all well-known companies. It is also clear that they had put it up in quick succession.

The list given above is significant also as it shows that Shakespeare had not confined his talent to any particular genre. Kyd and Marlowe had written only tragedies. Shakespeare, from the very beginning, was able to produce successful comedies (*The Two Gentlemen of Verona*), tragedies (*Titus Andronicus*) and histories in the field of drama itself, let alone that of sonnets and poems. Marlowe had already been killed by 1594 and Shakespeare had proved his versatility as well as stage-worthiness.

By this time he had joined the group of Lord Chamberlaine's Men, and had become an important member of it. This can be surmised because at this time the company had produced two plays at Court and the receipt of payment issued by the Royal Treasury contains the names of Shakespeare, Kempe and Burbage. Shakespeare remained in this company till the very end of his life. It was a case of a very happy symbiosis, for a company needed a good writer of its own in order to be in a state of continuous productivity, and a writer, of course, needed a company to produce his plays.

It is thought that he had paid a visit to Stratford at this time. Shakespeare's father, now in his sixties, was the head of a big family, surrounded by his children and grandchildren. Shakespeare himself was twenty-eight and his children were growing up—Susanna was nine and the twins were seven. It was time for Hamnet to start school. Shakespeare stayed in the bosom of his family for four months and it is thought that he wrote *Richard III* and *Venus and Adonis* during this visit. The poem was dedicated to the Earl of Southampton, the supposed "onlie begetter" of the sonnet-sequence.

Shakespeare was lucky to find a patron like the young Earl of Southampton, a handsome aristocrat about ten years junior to himself. He was a well-known patron of arts and, soon enough, a deep and intense friendship developed between them. The sonnets speak eloquently of this relationship, though there is no way of proving it in any other way. The Earl, not named anywhere in the sequence, is designated as Mr. W.H. in the Dedication and it is thought that these are the initials of Henry Wriothesely (The Earl of Southampton) in reversed order. The sonnets also describe a nameless Dark Lady with whom Shakespeare was in love. There follows a harrowing account of how Mr. W.H. and the Dark Lady together betrayed Shakespeare. How much of this is true cannot be known for sure but Shakespeare's intense love for Mr. W.H. is quite apparent. It has been expressed in the passionate tradition of Courtly Love.

Though the story told by the sonnets may not have much biographical relevance, it is quite true that Shakespeare enjoyed the patronage of the Earl of Southampton. He had dedicated the two narrative poems in addition to the sonnets to his patron. The Dedication in *The Rape of Lucrece* is instinct with the worshipful adoration he had towards Mr. W.H.:

> The love I dedicate to your Lordship is without end... what I have done is yours, what I have to do is yours, being part in all I have devoted yours.[9]

The patronage of the Earl gave his life the security that is so necessary for an artist. He was able to buy a share in his own company—the money, it is believed, being supplied by the Earl. In those times a poet had to have patronage in order to survive, unless, of course, he had some other source of income. Shakespeare was fortunate indeed. At this time Greene was languishing in poverty and sickness, whereas Shakespeare was buying property. A.L. Rowse remarks:

> It meant all the difference between the dreadful insecurity poor Greene had, and others, died of, and having firm ground under his feet.[10]

His company, having him for its writer, soon became the leading company in London. Apart from public performances, it gave thirty-two stagings in Queen Elizabeth's Court, a rare distinction for any theatrical company.

How prosperous and successful Shakespeare was can be understood only if we take a look at the literary perspective of the time. First of all, he was the only dramatist to survive the terrible havoc wrought by the Plague. Kyd was already dead at thirty-five years of age and Marlowe who was his most serious rival, was killed suddenly at a drunken brawl. Greene was dead at thirty-four years, and Peele would die in a few years. Lyly and Lodge had almost come to the end of their productivity. Nashe had turned to pamphlets in preference to plays. Ben Jonson, the only dramatist of a calibre like his own, had still not come. Shakespeare's star was in the ascendant at the moment.

The highly entertaining early comedies now poured forth. A successful man-about-town, he was enjoying life to the full and it is thought that Lord Berowne, the gayest and wittiest Lord in *Love's Labour's Lost* is, as Halliday describes, "a half-mocking and unconscious projection of himself." This was the year of 1595, and he was thirty years old, in the full vigour of energetic creativity. A literary mention of his name occurs in a poem by an Oxford undergraduate, one Henry Willoughby. He mentions Shakespeare as one who gives good advice about love-affairs. The poet particularly mentions his narrative poem:

> Yet Tarquin plucked his glistering grape
> And Shakespeare paints poor Lucrece's rape.[11]

In 1597, Shakespeare had the tragic experience of losing his only son and heir Hamnet. He was writing *King John* at the time. His father had, earlier, applied at the Herald's College for a coat-of-arms without any success and Shakespeare now pursued the matter. This would give his family the status of a gentleman—a matter of great importance in the feudal society of the time. This time the request was granted and our poet came back to London as a gentleman. He also bought New Place which was the second best house in Stratford, the first being the Town Hall. Stratford was no longer a little village, it had expanded into a big enough place to require a Town Hall. This gives an idea of Shakespeare's status.

By 1598, he was acknowledged as a master dramatist. A well-known document of the time named *Palladis Tamia* written by Francis Meres gives an eulogistic account of his works:

> ...the sweet wittie soule of Ovid lives in melliflueous and hony-tonged Shakespeare, witness his *Venus and Adonis,* his *Lucrece*, his sugred sonnets among his friends.[12]

This work gives a list of the plays that had been written and staged to date. This list is of great help to scholars in determining the dates of his works. Meres's attitude is a pointer to the high esteem in which Shakespeare was held. He asserts that Shakespeare is the contemporary equivalent of Terence and Plautus in comedy and of Seneca in tragedy.

Not only was Shakespeare acclaimed as the best dramatist of the time, but his company also got recognition. The Queen passed away in 1603 and King James VI of Scotland acceded to the throne of England as King James I. He took the lord Chamberlaine's men under his own patronage and the company was named as the King's Men. This was a coveted position—in fact the highest honour for any group. The members of the company would have the royal livery to wear and take part in all royal pageants and processions.

There are many records of Shakespeare's life from this point onwards. He had become well-settled in London. Legal documents prove that he went on changing his dwelling-place, staying at Bishopsgate in 1595, at Southwark in 1599, at Cripplegate in 1604. He bought a house at Blackfriars in 1613 though he did not occupy it. In 1602, he acquired a hundred and seven acres of land for farming and later in the same year he bought a cottage and a quarter acre of land. He continued to write for his company and also acted in it, for there existed a record that showed he had acted in Ben Jonson's *Sejanus*, a historical tragedy performed by his company in 1603.

He returned to Stratford in 1603 when there was another plague in London. His great tragedies were now produced. *Hamlet* was staged in 1602—the last play he wrote in the Elizabethan Age. In 1604, *Othello*, the first of his Jacobean plays, was performed at Court. The chronicles and the problem play were all written in the Jacobean Age. There is a great difference in spirit between the Elizabethan and the Jacobean Age. As Theodore Spencer has pointed out, the Renaissance optimism was succeeded by the Jacobean Age of conflict and pessimism. A sombre evaluation of life and person succeeded exuberance and enthusiasm. As Theodore Spencer has remarked:

> The earlier Renaissance had emphasized man's potentialities by comparing man with the angels; the later Renaissance emphasized their destruction by comparing man with the animals.[13]

The plays Shakespeare wrote at this time reflect this sombre attitude. The tragedies and the problem plays reflect the very spirit of the age in that they reflect upon the spirit of man and the nature of evil.

By now Shakespeare was spending his summers regularly at Stratford. In 1608, his mother passed away and his first grandchild was born. Both of these are events of moment, signifying the onset of age. In three more years (1611) he would leave London and settle at Stratford.

As the years passed he left the turbulent waters of the problem comedies and the tragedies behind him and emerged into the deep serenity of the last romances. The sonnet-sequence was published in 1609 and in 1611 (according to Irving Ribner and others) he retired to Stratford.

His connections with London, however, were not severed. He continued coming there on matters of business. For example he got the Blackfriar Gate House in 1613, and his name continued to appear in various documents. He kept up his connections with the stage for at the end of 1612 *The Tempest* was performed to celebrate a royal betrothal. It is said that he himself enacted the role of Prospero and blessed the couple.

His health was failing, though it is not well-known what he was suffering from. In 1616, his will was drawn up and can still be seen in Somerset House. This was in February and two months later, on 23rd April which was his birthday, he passed away at fifty-four years of age.

Many rich and complex symbols adorn his grave. There is a bust of himself with a quill in his hand, signifying that he was a writer. Corinthian columns stand at the sides with a cornice on them. The allegorical figures of Rest and of Labour adorn this cornice. His coat-of-arms is placed between these two figures and the whole thing is surmounted by a skull. There is a memorial tablet with a Latin couplet and a sextet in English. The grave itself bears an epitaph in the form of a quatrain. It is thought that this was written by the poet himself, though many scholars think that it is a bit too crude to have been his own work. This is how it runs:

> Good friend, for Jesus sake forbeare
> To dig the dust enclosed here!
>
> Blest be the man yt spares these stones
> And curst be he yt moves my bones.[14]

(B) SHAKESPEARE'S WORKS

A tentative scheme of Shakespeare's works has been drawn up by his critics and biographers. This has been based on contemporary documents like Henslowe's *Diary*, the Stationer's Register and others. These recorded the dates of the performances on stage, not of composition or of publications. Again, the dates of performances of many plays are not known and, to make the whole thing even more confusing, some of the plays like *Titus Andronicus* were published quite early, and some much later. Notwithstanding these difficulties, a scheme has been more or less agreed upon, though the stages cannot really be strictly demarcated.

Phase I

1591 — *The Comedy of Errors.*

'92 — *The Two Gentlemen of Verona, Henry VI, Parts I, II and III.*

1593 — *King Richard III, Romeo and Juliet, Venus and Adonis.*

Phase II

1594 — *The Rape of Lucrece, The Sonnets, Titus Andronicus King Richard II, A Midsummer Night's Dream, Love's Labour's Lost, King John, The Taming of the Shrew.*

'95 — *The Merchant of Venice.*

'97 — *Henry IV, Pt I.*

'98 — *Henry IV, Pt II, The Merry Wives of Windsor.*

'99 — *Henry V, Much Ado About Nothing, Julius Caesar.*

1600 — *As You Like It, Twelfth Night.*

Phase III

1602 — *Hamlet, Troilus and Cressida, All's Well That Ends Well.*

'04 — *Measure for Measure, Othello.*

'05 — *King Lear.*

'06 — *Macbeth.*

'07 — *Antony and Cleopatra.*

'08 — *Coriolanus, Timon of Athens, Pericles.*

Phase IV

1610 — *Cymbeline, The Winter's Tale, The Tempest.*

'11 — *Henry VIII.*

As this table shows, Shakespeare's career has been divided into four phases, though these are not mutually exclusive. Some critics, for example, think that all the works up to *Love's Labour's Lost* belong to the first phase, while some say that *Pericles* belongs to the fourth phase, not the third. These are matters of opinion. The first phase is known as the phase of Experiment or of Apprenticeship, from 1591 to 1594 or perhaps to 1595. At this time he was busy re-writing or revising plays that were already in existence—the best way for learning one's craft. He made frequent use of couplets and end-stopped lines at this time, as can be seen, for example, in *A Midsummer*

Night's Dream. Exuberant word-play can be seen in *Love's Labour's Lost*. The art of characterization has not developed yet, though he balances his characters against each other quite expertly.

The period of Development stretches from 1594-1595 to 1601. He produced the Golden Comedies (of which *As You Like It* is thought to be the best) and the Chronicles during this time. He has attained mastery over blank verse and has started to plumb the depths of the human mind in his portrayal of characters. The plots too, are handled with expertise.

1608 saw the end of the third phase. One can see a definite change of attitude in the work of this period. The witty and light-hearted characters are no longer there. Instead he had started looking evil in the face, evil in humanity as well as in Nature:

> The conflict between good and evil, ugliness and beauty, innocence and crime, purity and impurity, hope and disgust, love and hate, order and disorder, natural laws and the anarchy produced by the passions—all is resolved in Shakespeare's so-called "dark period" with an infinite despair.[15]

The Problem comedies and the Great tragedies belong to this period.

From now till 1612 is the last phase or the Romance period during which the last four Romances were written. Shakespeare has now achieved the wisdom that comes with age, a calm acceptance of the presence of evil as inevitable and a looking forward to the future with hope that a new generation will create a better world. Fluchère remarks:

> As his career draws to a close Shakespeare turned back to his youth, and his implicit theme is always that of fertility, resurrection, joy of life.[16]

The four Romances were followed by two more plays. Even up till the twentieth century there had been controvery about the chronicle play *King Henry VIII*. Nowadays, however, scholars agree in ascribing it to him. *The Two Noble Kinsmen*, it has always been known, was a work of collaboration with Fletcher.

The time has now come to cast a passing glance at his works. In the brief notes on his plays and poems that shall now be given, it has been tried to follow a roughly chronological order. As the dates of composition, performance and publication differ, it is difficult, not to say impossible, to he exact.

(C) BRIEF NOTES ON HIS WORKS

The Comedy of Errors

This play is his shortest, and was staged in 1594. There are many critics who think this to be the first of his works. The plot is from Plautus's rollicking comedy *The Menaechmuses* in which there is but one pair of twins and Shakespeare has doubled this. Consequently, the intrigues as well as the cases of mistaken identities have multiplied. The only theme that takes prominence is that of the relationship between husband and wife, which Shakespeare will deal with in detail later on, in *The Taming of the Shrew*.

The Two Gentlemen of Verona

This play is usually looked upon as the first of his romantic comedies. There are two pairs of lovers, two servants and two fathers. The characters, thus, are balanced against each other and make a symmetrical pattern. Conflict between love and friendship is the theme and the emphasis falls on friendship. There is also the theme of forgiveness and reconciliation that will occupy the poet so intensely in the last romances. Many features of his mature comedies, like crossed love, disguised heroines, exile, flight, etc. appear in this play. Julia is a precursor of Rosalind and Portia, and Silvia of Juliet.

Henry VI, Pts. I, II & III

This trilogy begins the chronicles that brought Shakespeare so much renown. He wrote ten such plays, including *Henry VIII*. These are not mere records of historical events. The serious issues of the duties and privileges of kings are also dealt with. He presented their human as well as ceremonial aspects, with all the pomp and pageantry it involved.

These plays were staged in 1592 and became so popular that the entire trilogy was performed three times in eight days Greene had referred to one of the lines (*vide* p. 22, *supra*). It presents a world of ferocity and ends in regicide.

Richard III

The early poetry of Shakespeare shows the influence of Marlowe. The *Henry VI* trilogy showed this quite clearly and in this play the influence can be seen not only in poetry but in characterisation as well. Richard III the hero is a Marlovian figure and the play too, is more like a tragedy than a history play. It is the second longest play of Shakespeare and extremely effective on the stage. Many critics group this play with the *Henry VI* trilogy and call the entire sequence a tetralogy. Yet the figure of the King dominates the play and his woeful fate makes the play a tragedy, evoking pity and terror.

Romeo and Juliet

This is one of his most popular tragedies, telling the story of star-crossed lovers. The hero and the heroine have become the archetypes of unfortunate lovers. This, like the Greek tragedies is a tragedy of fate, with family feud taking the place of fate. Shakespeare has not yet perfected his art of characterisation to the extent when it can be said that in his tragedies character is destiny. Instead he has followed the original story very closely. Some of the speeches and sense in it have become classics, particularly the Queen Mab speech by Merutio and the Balcony scene between the lovers.

Venus and Adonis

Narrative poems based on classical myths were very popular at that time and Shakespeare's became an instant hit. He took the story from Ovid, and the poem ran through ten or eleven editions in his own lifetime. He had many good models before him, particularly those by the University Wits. Narrative poetry was a new genre for him, but he shows himself a master at it. He has written it in sextains, i.e., a quatrain followed by a couplet. This is well-suited for narrative poetry and easier to handle than the nine-line form used by Spenser in his *Faerie Queene*, which Shakespeare must have read.

The Rape of Lucrece

This is the second of his long narrative poems and resembles *Venus and Adonis* in two other matters also—it is dedicated to the Earl of Southampton and is based on Ovid. This is a much more serious poem than the former one for Shakespeare tries to analyse the feeling of guilt in Tarquin. This psychological insight raises the poem above the light-hearted narratives that were fashionable at the time. Tarquin's conflicts of emotion raise him to tragic heights. Shakespeare has given proof of his poetic craft by using the rhyme royal form.

The Sonnets

This is a sequence of a hundred and fifty-four love-sonnets instinct with intense passion. They, as has been mentioned above (*vide* his Life, *supra*) are supposed to be autobiographical, depicting the relationship between himself and the Earl of Southampton whom he designates as Mr. W.H., "the onlie begetter" of these sonnets. The first 126 of the sonnets are addressed to him and the remaining to the equally famous Dark Lady, who was perhaps Mary Fitton, a maid of honour at Court. Usually Elizabethan love-sonnets were addressed to but one person, and Shakespeare's sequence is unique in that it explores a triangular relationship.

Titus Andronicus

This play is a Roman tragedy and also a revenge tragedy. It follows Seneca and Kyd and can be rightfully called a blood-and-thunder tragedy. It contains a well-known parody of a famous passage in Kyd's *The Spanish Tragedy*, and was extremely popular at that time.

Richard II

This play, unlike others, has a certain topical relevance. It reflects the political situation of the time so graphically that the Queen has been extremely annoyed and said, "I am Richard II, know ye that? This tragedy is played forty times in open streets and houses." The play shows the deposition of King Richard II and this was such a sensitive issue that the scene had to be omitted when the play was staged.

A Midsummer Night's Dream

This is undoubtedly the best among his early comedies. It has been very popular from the beginning and continues to be so. In it, for the first time, Shakespeare introduces the supernatural element in the characters of the fairy King and Queen and their attendants. The range of characters in the play, therefore, is wider than it had formerly been, and will be equalled only by *Tempest* at the end of his career. The story goes back to the pagan times of Greece.

Love's Labour's Lost

This play has always been notable for its witty dialogues. All the characters are witty, but Lord Berowne is the wittiest of all. The characters are all from high aristocracy, there being the French King, the Princess to whom he pays court, four courtiers and four ladies. In the subplot humbler characters have been introduced. As has been pointed out in the Life given above, the character of the happy-go-lucky, light hearted and witty Lord Berowne is supposed to be half-autobiographical. A passage by him, renouncing flowery and ornate diction, has become famous.

King John

This play is centred round the historical figure of King John, but, indirectly, it has a topical relevance as well. King John had waged a life-long battle with the Church of Rome and Queen Elizabeth had done the same. This had ultimately resulted in her excommunication by the Pope. Shakespeare has always avoided religious issues and this is the only play in which he has taken it up. In spite of this, the play is not a religious one. It is actually a highly patriotic play in which foreign policy is treated as the most important theme. The character of King John has been depicted with great insight. Shakespeare shows himself well able to deal with such issues.

The Taming of the Shrew

This play was performed in 1594 and has an Italian setting. The main characters, the hero and the heroine, have been strongly and effectively sketched in. The central theme is the relationship between husband and wife, both of them aiming at supremacy over the other, an extremely popular theme of his day. It is a most entertaining and stage-worthy play. Shakespeare, always mindful of neatly balancing his characters, has created another female character as foil for the shrew. This throws both the characters into relief. Shakespeare's talent for creating convincing characters can be clearly seen.

The Merchant of Venice

This is the first of his golden comedies. The merchant of the title should, according to custom, be the hero, but it is doubtful whether he can really be called so. As a matter of fact Shylock, the villain of the piece, is such a forceful character that he towers over everyone else. One of the most important female characters, Portia, is the heroine of this play. Shakespeare makes extensive and effective use of the Elizabethan convention of disguise, for each of the three female characters don male disguises, though for a very short time. He also shows full mastery over blank verse and poetic diction in this play, using different kinds of diction for different scenes and characters.

Henry IV—Pts. I & II

These two plays are the crowning achievements of English Chronicle plays. Sir John Falstaff has become the archetype of comic characters. Towards the end of the play Prince Hal accedes to the throne as King Henry V and leaving his days of jollity behind him, devotes himself to the duties of Kingship in earnest. He has to dissociate himself from the past and therefore rejects Falstaff who had been his boon companion all these days. Though his rejection of Falstaff is fully understandable and even commendable, the cruel manner of doing it creates a lasting impression in the audience Falstaff, however, has become immortal.

The Merry Wives of Windsor

Queene Elizabeth was so charmed by Falstaff that she ordered a play with "the fat knight in love" and Shakespeare produced this. This rollicking force begins at the point where *Henry IV, Pt. II* ends, i.e., with Falstaff's rejection. It is a highly entertaining and stage-worthy play but has not attracted serious critical attention. One feature of the play is significant: it seems that Shakespeare had poked fun at Ben Jonson's humour characters. Corporal Nym is a parody of such a character, for he uses the word "humour" in almost every sentence he speaks.

King Henry V

It has been affirmed by Shakespearean scholars that this play presents Shakespeare's concept of the ideal king. Kingship and patriotism are the twin themes of the play. Shakespeare deals with the historical battle of Agincourt in which the English won a resounding victory over the French. Shakespeare does not glorify war in a partisan manner, but, with the insight of a true poet, presents the positive as well as the negative side of war—bravery and endurance as well as death and suffering. Henry V shows himself as a strict but just King. Falstaff goes to Arthur's bosom in this play.

Much Ado About Nothing

This play is the second in the group of his four golden comedies. Like almost all Elizabethan comedies it has more than one plot and the theme is love. Shakespeare has presented the theme in two different ways. There is crude physical love which is based on appearances that prove to be deceptive. This aspect of love is presented in the Hero-Claudio plot. The Benedick-Beatrice plot takes up the theme of the rejection of married love that Shakespeare takes up repeatedly in his plays. As in the other comedies, the lovers gradually come to accept the social responsibilities of marriage though at first they are not conscious of this.

Julius Caesar

This play has been designated, along with *Coriolanus* and *Antony and Cleopatra*, as a Roman tragedy. The central theme of the play is the opposition of tyranny and liberty. It is a stern play with a stern plot which has but little of comedy in it. His characters, though historical, are all living and convincing human beings. He took the story from Lord North's translation of Plutarch's famous *Lives*. Shakespeare adapted many of the prose passages in this book into blank verse. This shows his resourcefulness. Supernatural elements are presented in the figure of Caesar's Ghost.

Twelfth Night

This play succeeds *As You Like It* which has not been mentioned here as it is the play under discussion *Twelfth Night* is the fourth and the last of the golden comedies. All the conventional elements of popular comedies are present in it: disguises, mistaken identities, the separation and re-union of siblings, etc. Shakespeare makes the plot even more complicated by making the separated siblings identical twins. A watered-down version of Falstaff is to be found in Sir Toby Belch, and one of the most remarkable jesters, Feste, is presented in this play. He is a highly accomplished jester, surpassed only by the unique Fool in *King Lear*. Viola is one of the most charming heroines of our poet.

Hamlet

This is the first of the four Great Tragedies and had been, for a long time, regarded as his best. It is his longest play. It is actually a revenge tragedy, but the crudities of Kyd are left far behind and the play is so sophisticated that this feature is often overlooked. It is the unique figure of Hamlet that overshadows every element of the play. He is a far more significant figure than merely a hero with the flaw of indecision.

Troilus and Cressida

This is the first of the problem comedies, and Shakespeare turns to Ancient Greece for his source material. These are all plays that deal with the most unattractive traits of human beings, presenting the seamy side of life. This particular play comes very near to a satire and gives a satirical, disillusioned treatment to the two themes of love and war.

All's Well That Ends Well

The second of the problem comedies, this play deals with the theme of the conflict between virtue and nobility. This is seen in the Bertram-Helena plot but there are several sub-themes, like the conflict between old and young generations. In this play Shakespeare is far less tolerant of the follies and vices of humanity than he had been earlier, as the braggart soldier Parolles shows.

Measure For Measure

Another problem comedy, this is a very serious play though like *As You Like It*, the merriest of the golden comedies, it ends with four marriages. The themes of justice and fidelity are the twin themes of the play. It contains one of the most charming songs of Shakespeare.

Othello

Hamlet was the last Elizabethan tragedy that Shakespeare had written, and *Othello* is the first of his Jacobean plays and the second of the four Great Tragedies. It has been called the *Romeo and Juliet* of his later phase and treats the theme of jealousy. One of his most important villains, Iago, comes in this play about whom the famous phrase "motiveless malignity" had been used by Coleridge.

King Lear

This is the play regarded at present as the greatest of his tragedies. It depicts, not merely the follies of King Lear and his tragic fate, but the predicaments of man himself in a cruel universe. The play has therefore been called a cosmic drama. A primitive legend has been transformed into a terrible tragedy that has the qualities of sublimity and universality in it. One of the unique characters in it is that of the Fool who serves many complex purposes. Dante's *Divine Comedy* is one of the works with which this play has been compared.

Macbeth

Shakespeare chose a story from Scottish history for this tragedy, thus paying a tribute to the Scottish king James I. It is well-known as the darkest and gloomiest of his tragedies. One of the most important characters in it is that of Lady Macbeth. He has also used supernatural elements in it.

Antony and Cleopatra

This is a sequel to *Julius Caesar*, though it is totally different in theme. It is the theme of love that he has taken up here. The character of Cleopatra dominates the play. It is so complex that it has variously been called a history, a symphony, a political play and a Roman tragedy.

Coriolanus

This is a political Roman tragedy, the last of his tragedies. Critics usually group it with the two other Roman tragedies, *Julius Caesar* and *Antony* and *Cleopatra*. The hero is so intrinsically noble that he is in conflict with society and therefore society rejects him. This brings about his tragic end.

Timon of Athens

Though this is a five-act problem comedy, it is generally felt that this is not a complete play. It ends with the hero's (who is a misanthrope) from society, but this is no fitting end and leaves a feeling of incompleteness in the mind of the reader.

PERICLES, CYMBELINE

THE WINTER'S TALE, THE TEMPEST

This group is known as the last Romances and the same theme, repeatedly, occurs in them. This is the theme of sin, repentance and forgiveness. Alongside this runs the theme of a tainted and chastened older generation handing the future over to a newer, purer younger generation. *The Tempest* is his last play, acted to celebrate a royal betrothal. Shakespeare had acted in the role of Prospero and blessed the royal couple. Prospero's renunciation is thought to be Shakespeare's farewell to the theatre.

Henry VIII

Modern scholars agree in attributing this play to Shakespeare though this had been a matter of controversy for a long time. It takes up the theme of patience in adversity. Not only does the King himself learn patience but so do the other characters as well. It ends with an affirmation of the continuity of life.

The Two Noble Kinsmen

This is a work of collaboration with Fletcher. Shakespeare wrote the major parts of Act I and also parts of Acts III and V. Many of his contemporaries had collaborated with others, but this is the only such work of Shakespeare. When Fletcher introduced a rather vulgar sub-plot Shakespeare left off working with him. The story is taken from Chaucer.

REFERENCES

1. The dates for these works have been taken from *The New Caxton Encyclopaedia*, London, Caxton Pubs. Ltd., 1982, 20 Vols.
2. Cited in Halliday, F.E., *The Life of Shakespeare*. London, Gerald Duckworth & Co. Ltd., 1961, p. 20.
3. *As You Like It*, Act II, scene vii, ll. 145-47, p. 38. Ware, Wordsworth Classics, 1993.
4. Ribner, Irving, *William Shakespeare: Life, Times and Theatre*, London, John Wiley and Sons Inc., 1969, pp. 38-39.
5. Craig, H., *op. cit.*, p. 52, Citation.
6. Halliday, F.E., *op. cit.*, p. 60.
7. Quoted in Ribner, I., *op. cit.*, p. 45.
8. Quoted in Rowse, A.L., *William Shakespeare: A Biography*, London, Macmillan & Co. Ltd., 1963, p. 100.
9. Quoted in Halliday, *op. cit.*, pp. 102-03.
10. Rowse, A.L., *op. cit.*, p. 201.
11. Halliday, *op. cit.*, p. 118.
12. *Ibid.*, p. 138, Ribner, *op. cit.*, p. 52 and many others.
13. Spencer, Theodore, *Shakespeare and the Nature of Man*. New York, The Macmillan Company, 1945, p. 49.
14. Quoted in Ribner, *op. cit.*, p. 64, and by many others.
15. Fluchère, H., *Shakespeare*, London, Longman & Green, 1953, p. 54.
16. *Ibid.*, p. 265.

3

The Story and the Genre

(A) THE STORY IN BRIEF

As You Like It is the story, mainly of the attractive and witty princess Rosalind who, at first dogged by misfortune is, at the end of the play, united with her beloved Orlando who, like her, had undergone vicissitudes of fortune. Her father, the Duke had been banished from the kingdom that was rightfully his by his usurping brother Frederick. He, with some loyal followers, has, when the play opens, taken refuge in the forest of Arden. Rosalind, his daughter, however, has not accompanied him. Frederick's daughter Celia loves Rosalind so much that she cannot live without her, so Rosalind is staying with her.

The hero Orlando is similarly subjected to adverse circumstances. In his case it is his elder brother Oliver who maltreats him. Being the eldest, Oliver has inherited his father's property. Sir Rowland de Boys, who had three sons, had placed the two younger sons under Oliver's care. Oliver has not accorded Orlando the education that is needed for noblemen, nor has he given him the money left to him by his father. Orlando complains:

> ...he lets me feed with his hinds, bars me the place of a brother and, as much as in him lies, mines my gentility with my education.[1]

Duke Frederick has arranged for a wrestling match and, knowing that Orlando means to appear at it, Oliver conspires with Charles, the Duke's wrestler, to kill him. Orlando, however, beats Charles. It is during this wrestling-match that Orlando and Rosalind meet and fall deeply in love with each other Frederick, as soon as he comes to know that Orlando is the son of Sir Rowland who was an intimate friend of Rosalind's father, becomes highly prejudiced against him. Moreover, when Orlando comes home his faithful servant Old Adam informs him that there is a plot to kill him. Orlando decides to leave his home. Adam goes with him.

Rosalind fares no better. Duke Frederick, without any reason, banishes her from the kingdom. She decides to go to the forest of Arden to seek out her father and Celia begs to accompany her. For the sake of convenience and safety, they decide to disguise themselves. Rosalind will be a shepherd with the name of Ganymede and Celia her sister, with the name of Aliena. Thus in this play two female characters adopt the disguise of males. This was a very popular Elizabethan convention. Touchstone the court-jester is also to go with them.

The forest of Arden is a very pleasant place—an ideal pastoral background for the play. It is here that the rest of the play takes place. The dispossessed Duke (Rosalind's father) stays here with a few followers two of whom are named, Jaques and Amiens. The former is a melancholy man, one of the well-known figures of Elizabethan drama. They all lead a simple, happy life. The Duke, instead of being sad and downcast, is not only happy himself, but encourages his followers to enjoy this life in the lap of nature:

> Hath not old custom made this life more sweet
> Than that of painted pomp? Are not these woods
> More free from peril than the envious court?[2]

Rosalind, Celia and Touchstone reach the forest. They meet Corin, an old shepherd who tells them of a cottage and a flock of sheep which is for sale. They give him the money to buy all these and decide to stay in the cottage at the outskirts of the forest. Orlando and Adam also finally reach the forest and join the Duke's retinue.

Orlando, deeply in love with Rosalind, writes poems to her and pins them to trees which Rosalind finds and reads. When they meet, however, Orlando does not recognize them as they are in disguise. Rosalind proposes to cure him of love by pretending to him to be Rosalind (he knows her as Ganymede the shepherd-boy). He will then court her and this will gradually cure him. Orlando agrees thinking it to be good sport to imagine a young Shepherd to be a princess.

Meanwhile Touchstone has been attracted towards Audrey, a village girl. There is another pair of lovers, for Silvius a shepherd loves Phoebe a shepherdess. There are thus three pairs of lovers now in the forest. Phoebe does not respond to Silvius's courting favourably and repulses him. Rosalind advises her to take him, for he is a sincere lover and a good man:

> But mistress, know yourself—down on your knees
> And thank heaven, fasting, for a good man's love.[3]

Phoebe, however is attracted towards her, taking her to be a shepherd. This gives rise to complications, for she writes a love-letter to Rosalind and makes Silvius carry it to her. Rosalind tells Silvius that Phoebe has made a fool of him and advises him to turn away from her. Their conversation is interrupted by the entrance of Oliver, the elder brother of Orlando who had forced him to flee.

Oliver's land and property had been confiscated by Duke Frederick and he too had taken refuge in the forest. He tells Rosalind and Celia a strange story. He was asleep under a tree and a snake was going to bite him when Orlando appeared on the spot which made the snake glide away. A hungry lioness, however, was waiting for Oliver to wake up. Orlando fought the lioness and because of his injuries he could not keep his appointment with Rosalind. So he has sent her his handkerchief stained with his blood.

The sight of the handkerchief makes Rosalind faint and as Oliver and Celia take her home they fall in love with each other. Thus, we have a fourth pair of lovers. This love is so deep that Oliver has decided to give up city life and to continue living in the forest as a shepherd, giving all his property to Orlando. It is decided that he and Celia will get married the next day.

Rosalind then comes to meet Orlando and tells him she has magical powers and can bring Rosalind to him. She promises that he shall marry Rosalind when Oliver marries Celia. Silvius and Phoebe then enter and after some conversation Rosalind tells them to meet her the next day. Audrey and Touchstone also have decided to marry the next day.

Thus all the characters assemble the next day and Rosalind, still in disguise, makes the Duke and Orlando promise that Orlando shall marry Rosalind if she is brought there. She then makes Phoebe promise that she shall marry Silvius if she refuses to marry Ganymede. Then the two of them withdraw and reappear dressed in their proper clothes.

There is a masque in which Hymen the god of marriage appears with a train of followers. All confusions are resolved at the entrance of the two girls and now four marriages can take place. The play however, ends even more happily for everyone concerned because Jaques de Boyes, the second son of Sir Rowland (Oliver being the first and Orlando the third) arrives with a message. Duke Frederick who was coming to the forest with the intention of killing the elder Duke (Rosalind's father) had met a hermit at the edge of the forest. A conversation with the hermit had brought about a total change of heart and now he has decided to renounce the world and lead the life of a hermit. So the crown and all the land he had usurped from the Duke comes back to him.

Now everyone prepares to go back to the erstwhile lost kingdom and the Duke orders music to be played so that the marriage can be celebrated before they leave the forest. Here Jaques declares that he would join Duke Frederick in the forest and with him lead the life of a hermit. So he leaves the stage and the dancing begins.

At the end there is an Epilogue spoken by Rosalind in which she says that the play is a light entertainment. She addresses the audience and asks the men to love the play as they love their women and she asks the women to love the play as they love their men. It is a very charming Epilogue and leaves the impression of wit and happiness—a fitting end to a witty and happy play, for this is the sunniest of all the golden comedies.

(B) THE GENRE OF THE PLAY

Shakespeare's plays are so complex that usually there are several interpretations of the many different aspects of his plays. The plot, the characters, the imagery, etc. have all been explained in many ways by many critics. The genre is an aspect over which there is great variety of critical opinions. So far as *As You Like It* goes, however, there has not been much speculation on this head. The play is a romantic comedy with pastoral elements in it. As it is, Shakespeare's plays have been put into different groups, of which the group of golden comedies is one. This contains four plays—*The Merchant Of Venice*, *Much Ado About Nothing*, *As You Like It* and *Twelfth Night*. The golden comedies is but one of the names, they are also known as the romantic comedies, festive comedies, happy comedies, etc.

(i) Romantic Comedy

The main theme in such plays is that of love. Shakespeare has written many of these. The early comedies (*Love's Labour's Lost,* etc.) are all romantic comedies, and so are the golden comedies. Remarking on this aspect, H.B. Charlton has pointed out that, first of all, it is this aspect that sets English comedies apart from classical plays, whether Greek or Latin:

> Romantic comedy is pre-eminently the comedy of love. It is its specific pre-occupation with wooing which distinguishes it most markedly from classical or roman comedies.[4]

The element of love, as presented by the writers, has certain distinctive features. The classical comedies treat the theme in a light-hearted manner. Love-intrigues in them are related more with the plot than to the characters, or even the theme. But in these romantic comedies a girl has to be courted in a very serious manner. She is to be won and cherished for ever afterwards. Her love and her hand are treasures that can be won with great difficulty. Love has, instead of being a light-hearted affair, become a noble and intense emotion, transforming the lover into a better and nobler person, worthy of the girl's devotion.

This change in the attitude to love and women brought about a drastic change in comedy itself. The ideas of courtly love and the ideals of chivalry changed the very nature of romantic comedy:

> Dante had transmuted womankind for men. He had opened their eyes to the image of woman whose coming is as from heaven to reveal a miracle.[5]

This is the attitude, that of chivalric love, that is to be found in Elizabethan romantic comedy. Referring specially to Shakespearean comedies, he traces Shakespeare's developing ability to combine the comic element with the romantic and turning to the golden comedies he remarks that they are:

> ...his happiest expression of the characteristically Elizabethan kind of romantic comedy, the plays in which he most fully satisfied the curiously Elizabethan aesthetic demand for a drama which would gratify both the romantic and the comic instincts of its audience.[6]

As a matter of fact, H.B. Charlton regards *As You Like It* as the very consummation of Shakespeare's art of constructing romantic comedies. Love is definitely the central theme of the play (*vide* Ch. 5, Major Themes, *infra*). We have love of many different kinds. For example there is romantic love in the courtly tradition between Orlando and Rosalind, a very down-to-earth kind of love between Touchstone and Audrey and pastoral love between Silvius and Phoebe. In the happy world of the forest of Arden, love motivates the characters and grows to maturity as in no other play of Shakespeare. John Dover Wilson points out:

> In the shimmering air of Romance which the inhabitants of Arden breathe, love is the main industry.[7]

This opinion has hardly been deviated from. The later critics all agree that this play is the very epitome of romantic comedy. Following in the footsteps of Charlton Phialas, a much later critic, studying the development of Shakespeare's romantic comedies, comes to the conclusion:

> With *As You Like It* Shakespeare reached a significant milestone in his career as a comic dramatist and here his

> mode of romantic comedy achieved so successful a form that further development seemed impossible.[8]

Phialas takes a very serious view of romantic comedy. According to him these plays of Shakespeare are anything but pure entertainment. Instead they explain the psychological need for reaching an ideal and mature attitude to love and life. Shakespeare has, in the person of Rosalind, harmoniously brought the element of idealized pastoral love and psychological realities together (*vide* Ch. 6, Rosalind's character, *infra*).

(ii) Pastoral Comedy

In addition to being a romantic comedy, the play under discussion is also a pastoral comedy, as the majority of the events in it take place in the pastoral environs of the forest of Arden. It is, thus, often called a pastoral romance. Baker, one of the earliest critics labels it as such:

> It is, perhaps, the truest pastoral drama that ever was written.[9]

This is perfectly justified for, as has been pointed out, except for the first three scenes, the entire play is located in the forest. With the change of location the entire tone of the play undergoes a definite change. The reader becomes conscious of this just as he does when the location changes in, for example, *A Midsummer Night's Dream*. This happens in Act II, and the note of the pastoral is stressed by the Duke in the very first lines:

> Now, my co-mates and brothers in exile
> Hath not old custom made this life more sweet.
> Than that of painted pomp? Are not these woods
> More free from peril than the envious court?
> Here feel we not the penalty of Adam,
> The seasons' difference?[10]

As the play proceeds, the difference between the artificiality of courtly life and the simplicity of pastoral life is repeatedly contrasted and pointed out. Not only is the pastoral life free from all the worries and anxieties typical of courtly life, it is also a life that strengthens the moral fibre. Mother nature gives infinite pleasure to her children and teaches valuable lessons as well:

> And this our life, exempt from public haunt,
> Finds tongues in trees, books in the running brooks,
> Sermons in stones, and good in everything.[11]

Pastoral surroundings assume the existence of shepherds and Shakespeare gives us real shepherds as well as pretended ones. Corin and Silvius are genuine shepherds and Phoebe a genuine, fully convincing shepherdess. On the other hand, Rosalind and Celia who have disguised themselves as such are not real shepherds. It must not, however, be forgotten that as they approach the outskirts of the forest they meet Corin and Rosalind makes him buy, on their behalf, the cottage, the pasture and the flock he has been tending. Thus, though they themselves are not genuine shepherds they are the owners of a pasture and a flock. For some time they are able to leave the cares of the court and live like shepherds, just like the Duke.

There are many interesting features of the pastoral that Shakespeare has presented here. The pastoral world, like the Garden of Eden (which is the ideal pastoral world) is one in which pure innocence reigns. Those who enter it from the outer world and are already polluted by all the corruptions of the outside world can yet achieve innocence when they come within. The Duke takes refuge in the forest and as he passes his days he becomes purified—a nobler and more virtuous person. The mortification of losing his kingdom, the pain of being betrayed by his brother, the humiliation of being driven out of his kingdom, all these are gradually washed away by benevolent nature and finally he becomes able even to praise his misfortune so that he finds that even the inclemencies of weather are uplifting in their total and ultimate effects:

> Sweet are the uses of adversity,
> Which like the toad, ugly and venomous
> Wears yet a precious jewel in his head.[12]

Not only do the pastoral surroundings spread their influence over the Duke, but over natures that are far, far worse. Frederick and Oliver are both villains and both undergo changes of heart on reaching the forest. The former comes to kill the Duke but it is his own evil nature that is destroyed and he becomes a different man. Very much the same happens to Oliver, Orlando's evil brother, who also undergoes a change of heart. He, after being saved by Orlando, is ashamed of himself:

> 'Twas I, but 'tis not I: I do not shame
> To tell you what I was, since my conversion
> So sweetly tastes, being the thing I am.[13]

Not only is his evil nature purified but he falls in love with Aliena. This pure and true love is of great influence. From an arrogant ill-natured man he becomes a humble lover. It is as if the pastoral surrounding, like a benevolent spirit, transforms evil into good and misery into joy.

There are many learned discussions of the pastoral aspect of the play. Some critics, for example, think that the dramatist presents a satirical version of the pastoral, mocking at the artificial conditions prevailing in the genre of pastoral poetry and drama. John Dover Wilson thinks that the play is:

> ...at once an exquisite essay in the pastoral manner and a sly criticism of it.[14]

This is a superficial treatment of this aspect of the play. A far more serious view is taken by Phialas, a later critic who, after driving home the point that shepherds and shepherdesses appear for the first time in Shakespeare in this play, points out that the dramatist had made use of the pastoral convention with a particular purpose in mind. He deliberately juxtaposes three different worlds in it: (1) the world of "literary pastoralism" (2) the "pastoralism of fashionable Elizabethans" and in addition (3) "the real world of the country." There is conflict between these but this conflict is assimilated within the framework of romantic comedies.[15] He regards the play as a romantic comedy but gives great importance to the pastoral element.

Thus, some regard the play as a parody of pastoral comedies, some as a satirical exposition of the pastoral and some as a means for explaining deeper psychological truths. Perceiving these factors, Hazlitt with his usual acuteness had remarked about the characters:

> Within the sequestered and romantic glades of the forest of Arden, they do find leisure to be good and wise or to play the fool and fall in love.[16]

(iii) Green World Comedy

This interpretation of the play's genre is dependent upon the pastoral element, but is different enough to be considered on its own. Northrop Frye points out the difference between "drama of the green world" and that of the ordinary world. In this kind of play the action begins in the common day-to-day world, then moves forward into a "green world" where it reaches a happy conclusion and is finally brought back to the normal world. The dramatist compares and contrasts the two worlds. Very much the same happens in *A Midsummer Night's Dream*, but in that play the characters' return to the old normal world is given in detail, whereas in this play it is only hinted at.

Such green world comedies, to which group *The Two Gentlemen of Verona A Midsummer Night's Dream*, *The Merchant of Venice* also belong, have their own peculiar plot-structures and characters. Usually, the hero and the heroine find themselves opposed by a figure of power and authority and take refuge in the green world that lies beyond the bounds of court as in *As You Like It* or the city as in *A Midsummer Night's Dream*. Then this world poses its own rules and presents obstacles to be overcome by the characters. Orlando has to show the true nobility of his nature by caring for his old servant and later by saving the life of Oliver. The Duke and his followers have to undergo many hardships and accept everything stoically. Rosalind has to pose as a shepherd-boy, Celia has to give up her home and inheritance.

Sherman Hawkins, analyzing the implications of this interpretation remarks:

> Frye's green-world theory seems to me both true and useful; it isolates a recurring psychological and mythic pattern in Shakespeare's comedies.[17]

(iv) A Pure Comedy

This is the label given to the play by Helen Gardner. She differentiates "pure comedy" from "corrupt or satirical comedy":

> The great symbol of pure comedy is marriage by which the world is renewed and its endings are always instinct with a sense of fresh beginnings.[18]

She further argues that comedy is the very image of the flow of human life. It deals with sudden changes of mind and surprises. Thus the sudden falling in love of Orlando-Rosalind, the sudden changes of mind of Duke Frederick when he rebuffs Orlando, and again when he banishes Rosalind and most of all when he undergoes the conversion at the end, are all authentic material for comedy. Shakespeare gives a world conducive to the benign flow of what Rosalind calls "the full stream of the world." The most important evidence of this are the changes he made in the original story. For example, Charles the wrestler kills the young men who challenge him in the romance by Lodge, but Shakespeare lets them go with broken ribs. Again in the source story the wicked Duke is killed in a battle, but our poet makes him undergo a conversion. In comedy evil exists but does not triumph, instead it is life that triumphs and our play celebrates this triumph of life. It does not seek to reform either man or nature (as is done in "corrupt comedy") but goes onwards, taking everything with it.

(v) An Escape Play

This is the view held by John Dover Wilson. There are so many complexities in the play that it has confused the critics themselves. John Dover Wilson for example, regards it as a romantic comedy, a pastoral comedy, a criticism of the pastoral convention, an escape-play and also as a pattern play (*see below*). He gives a discussion of the pastoral element in it and points out how Shakespeare makes a parody of conventional pastoralism and at the some time presents true and ideal love through the character of the hero and the heroine. It is a play in which Shakespeare's main characters escape out of the court into a forest, that is, out of an artificial life into an innocent, natural life. Some of the characters adjust themselves so well in it that the escape, instead of being temporary, becomes a permanent one. Frederick becomes a hermit and so does Jaques. Oliver renounces his land and becomes, with his wife, a shepherd. The Duke Orlando and Rosalind escape temporarily.

At the close of the play they go back to the Court. It is perhaps for this reason that Dover Wilson declares:

> *As You Like It* is Shakespeare's Arcadia, his escape-play; it is also Shakespeare's criticism of Arcadia and escape-literature.[19]

(vi) A Pattern Play

This, as the one given above, is one of the views of John Dover Wilson. He points out that *As You Like It*, unlike *Much Ado About Nothing* and *Twelfth Night*, "does not act itself" for it does not have any of those extremely popular scenes that are so successful on-stage. For example, the scene in which Malvolio reads Maria's letter in *Twelfth Night* is a:

> ...scene which is foolproof and cannot fail with an audience, however stupidly put on. But *As You Like It* belongs to the same type of comedy as *Love's Labour's Lost*.[20]

Instead of having such hilarious scenes, *As You Like It* contains situations in which men holding opposing points to view meet and talk. This highlights an intellectual quality in the play—a quality which requires thoughtful acting. There are different patterns of speech in these discussions between different characters. For example, when Amiens and Jaques talk about the song "under the greenwood tree", they talk very differently to how Corin the shepherd and Touchstone the jester talk about the differences between a courtly and a pastoral life. Orlando with his idealized love meets Rosalind, then she proposes to cure him of it. In all these cases there are encounters between characters who hold views contrary to each other's. Thus he declares:

> It is made up of encounters between opposed points of view and of the talk that results therefrom. In other words it is a pattern play and demands brains in the true performing of it.[21]

These are some of the views on the genre of the play. The above discussion will inform the serious student that the play is basically a romantic play with strong pastoral elements in it, but there are many views about the treatment of the element of love and of the pastoral in it. Keeping both of these features in mind, H. Gardner, for example, calls it a Mozartian comedy:

> *As You Like It* is the most refined and exquisite of the comedies. It is Shakespeare's most Mozartian comedy.[22]

L.S. Champion calls this play a comedy of identity in which action is of less importance than character:

> Shakespeare rejects comedy based upon action alone and moves towards the development of character.[23]

Raymond Adlam, again, finds elements of a concert in it.[24] All these and other views, serve to emphasize the rich complexity of the play.

REFERENCES

1. *As You Like It*, Ware Wordsworth Classics, 1993. Act I, scene i, lines 17-19, p. 3. All further quotations from the text will be from this edition, unless otherwise indicated.
2. Act II, sc. i, ll. 2-4, p. 22.
3. Act III, sc. v, ll. 57-58, p. 61.
4. Charlton, H.B., *Shakespearean Comedy*, London, Methuen & Co. Ltd., University pbk, no date, p. 21.
5. *Ibid.*, p. 21.
6. *Ibid.*, p. 266.
7. Wilson, John Dover, *Shakespeare's Happy Comedies*, London, Faber paper-covered edn., no date, p. 158.
8. Phialas, P.G., *Shakespeare's Romantic Comedies: The Development of their Form and Meaning*. Chapel Hill, The Univ. of N. Carolina Press, 1966, p. 209.
9. Baker, David Erskine, in Brown, John Russell, ed., *Shakespeare: Much Ado About Nothing* and *As You Like It: A Casebook*, London, Macmillan, 1979, p. 24.
10. Act II, sc. i, ll. 1-6, p. 22.
11. Act II, sc. i, ll. 15-17, p. 22.
12. Act II, sc. i, ll. 12-14, p. 22.
13. Act IV, sc. iii, ll. 135-37, p. 75.
14. Wilson, J.D., *op. cit.*, p. 146.
15. Phialas, P.G., *op. cit.*, p. 219.
16. Brown, J.R., *op. cit.*, p. 34.

17. Hawkins Sherman, *The Two Worlds of Shakespearean Comedy* in Brown, J.R., *op. cit.*, p. 51.
18. Gardner, Helen, *Let the Forest Judge*, *ibid.*, p. 153.
19. Wilson, J. Dover, *op. cit.*, p. 162.
20. *Ibid.*, p. 159.
21. *Ibid.*
22. Gardner, Helen, *Let the Forest Judge*, in Brown, John Russel, *op. cit.*, p. 149.
23. Champion, L.S., *The Evolution of Shakespeare's Comedy: A Study in Dramatic Perspectives*, Harvard, the University Press, 1970, p. 61.
24. Adlam, Raymond, *Shakespeare: As You Like It.* Notes on Literature. Issued by the British Council, Number 138, January 1973, London, p. 2.

4

A Scene-wise Analysis of the Play

Act I, Scene i

This, the first scene of the play, introduces us to the hero. Sometimes in our poet's works certain characters gain so much prominence that it becomes difficult to identify the hero. For example in *The Merchant of Venice* it is difficult to say who the hero of the play is. There is no such difficulty here. Orlando is the undisputed hero of it.

He is not only discontented with his present situation in life, he is also very angry. Here in this speech he tells us how Orlando is the youngest son of Sir Rowland de Boys who has died. We are told he left a thousand crowns to Orlando, with an injunction on his eldest son Oliver, to bring him up as befits the son of an aristocrat. Oliver has not honoured his father's wishes and has neglected his brother shamefully:

> he lets me feed with his hinds, bars me the place of a brother and, as much as in him lies, mines my gentility with my education.[1]

Orlando, however, is not entirely alone, for he has Adam, his father's old servant, who loves him and is loyal to him, giving him the sympathy he needs.

A few minutes later Oliver comes in and soon enough a quarrel springs up. Oliver hits Orlando and the latter takes him by the throat. He tells Oliver that either he must get the education he is entitled to, or the thousand crowns left by his father. Oliver agrees to do the latter and as soon as he is alone, says that he will not give Orlando the money. Then he calls Charles who is the wrestler at Duke Frederick's court.

He (and the audience) learn from Charles that the old Duke has been banished by the treacherous younger brother and has gone, with a few followers, to the forest of Arden. His daughter Rosalind is staying in the palace, for Frederick's daughter Celia (her cousin) love each other so much that Celia cannot live without her. He also tells Oliver that he has come to know that his brother is going to participate in a wrestling-match to be held the next day. Oliver quickly seizes the chance to hint clearly that he will be only too pleased if Charles not only defeats but kills him. So Orlando's future is taken care of and as soon as Charles goes away Oliver tell us the reason for his hatred for Orlando: it is only jealousy:

> ...for my soul, (yet I know not why) hates nothing more than he...so much in the heart of the world and especially of my own people, who best know him, that I am altogether misprized.[2]

There are many things to be noted about this scene. First of all it is entirely in prose. It must be remembered that Elizabethan plays were usually written in a mixture of verse and prose. The noble characters spoke in verse and others in prose. In this scene there are two noble ones but they speak in prose because very often the noble characters did so when speaking to humble ones. But in this scene Shakespeare gives prose to the two brothers even when speaking to each other. This is because they are quarrelling and such occasions do not merit poetry.

As the scene is the first, it cannot be linked to any foregoing scene in the play but only to later ones. Shakespeare always provides issues reaching forwards and backwards linking scenes to one another. This scene looks forward to the next scene in which the wrestling-match is going to take place.

It is an extremely functional scene because in it the hero is introduced and the element of fraternal enmity is brought in. This is a motif that occurs again and again. In *The Tempest* also there is enmity between prospero and his brother Antonio. In this play also enmity and consequent betrayal are presented twice—Oliver betrays Orlando, and the Duke is betrayed by Frederick his brother. There are parallels between *Tempest* and this play in that in both the younger brother turns out to be a usurper and drives away the older one. All these are highly negative aspects of humanity, but Shakespeare also shows the positive aspect in Adam's loyalty to Orlando.

Shakespeare has very cleverly prepared the audience for Orlando's winning the wrestling-match. He is presented as a very strong young man, for he takes Oliver by the throat and Oliver cannot free himself. Though Charles is a professional wrestler, we feel that Orlando also has some hope.

Shakespeare also prepares us for the peaceful world of the forest where Duke Senior has gone. Charles describes it as a golden world:

> ...there they love like the old Rohin Hood of England: they say many young gentlemen flock to him everyday and fleet the time carelessly as they did in the golden world.[3]

As far as construction goes the scene can be neatly divided into two equal halves. The first part lasts till l. 83 when Orlando and Adam leave the stage. The second part begins with the entrance of Dennis, a servant who calls Charles. The scene consists of 162 lines and so the two halves of the scene are balanced equally. Orlando's conversation in the beginning with Adam can also be looked upon as being in the nature of a Prologue.

Act I, Scene ii

The heroine Rosalind is brought on the stage and so is her cousin Celia. It opens with a dialogue between the two cousins which is instinct with their generous unselfish love for each other. Then Touchstone the clown approaches them bringing a summons from Duke Frederick. Instead of going, however, they continue talking and after a witty dialogue Le Beau, one of the courtiers, enters to tell them that they have lost much in the way of entertainment for the wrestling-match had begun. Now the entire court was coming to this place for the rest of the match will take place here. Charles has already defeated three young men.

Duke Frederick enters with his retinue. While the place for the match is being prepared Frederick asks the two girls to try and dissuade Orlando from fighting Charles. So Orlando is called and the hero and the heroine meet for the first time. Both of the girls try to prevent Orlando fighting Charles, but Orlando is adamant in his determination.

The match begins and Orlando defeats Charles. Duke Frederick is pleased and asks Orlando his name. As soon as he hears the name of his father all his geniality evaporates, for he regarded Sir Rowland as his enemy, and he goes away without rewarding Orlando.

The two girls and Orlando are now on the stage. They congratulate him and Rosalind gives him her own chain. Both of them have fallen deeply in love with each other. Orlando is rendered speechless, and is surprised at himself:

> What passion hangs these weights
> I cannot speak to her[4] upon my tongue?

By this time Rosalind and Celia have both gone and Le Beau comes and gives him friendly advice. Duke Frederic, instead of having rewarded him for winning the match, had repulsed him. Orlando should be feeling repulsed and disappointed. This is not the case, however, for Orlando is totally occupied with his state of being in love. Everything else but Rosalind is driven out of his mind. Le Beau, not knowing this, has sympathy for him:

> Albeit you have deserved
> High commendation, true applause and love,
> Yet such is now the Duke's condition,
> That he misconstrues all that you have done.[5]

He counsels Orlando to go quickly away. Orlando thanks him and asks about Rosalind. Le Beau tells him about Rosalind's position in the palace and also that the Duke is displeased with her. They bid each other goodbye and the scene ends.

This scene is a mixture of prose and verse. In the beginning when Rosalind and Celia are talking, they do so in prose and this is continued till much more than half the scene is over. It is only towards the end, with l. 210 that verse begins. Thereafter, the rest of the scene is in poetry. At the very end there is a couplet. Such couplets sum up the scene or express a moral and are known as Senecan couplets or "sententiae."

The scene is firmly linked with the former and the later ones in that the wrestling-match has already been anticipated in the preceding scene. It looks forward to the later scene in two different ways. First of al Le Beau mentions the fact that Frederick is angry with Rosalind and this is borne out by the next scene. Secondly in Act II, sc. iii Orlando comes home only to be forced to flee, for Adam tells him that Oliver means to kill him. This too is anticipated here in the last lines.

The main event of the scene is not the fight but the falling in love of Rosalind and Orlando. Though sudden, it is an intense and enduring love. The state of Rosalind's mind is not as clearly expressed as Orlando's but can easily be surmised. There is no doubt about Orlando's.

Le Beau's account of Frederick's character is of significance as it makes it clear that he is of rather unstable mood, and is unpredictable. He takes a sudden dislike to Orlando and has, without any reason, turned against his niece. The later behaviour of the Duke is supported by these facts. Le Beau mentions that he is "humorous", that is, he is predominated by a certain emotion. The "humour" character is well-known in these plays though Shakespeare rarely deals with them.

The scene can be divided into three parts. Part one lasts till Duke Frederick enters (ll. 1-138), part two comprises the match (ll. 139-209) and then the third part follows. This last part is sharply set apart from the rest of the scene by being written in verse. The most important event of the play, the falling in love of the hero and the heroine, is depicted in this part, and it is fitting that it should be rendered in poetry.

The wrestling-match serves two important purposes. It brings the hero and the heroine together and secondly it provides the element of spectacle (*opsis*) which according to Aristotle is one of the elements of drama.

Act I, Scene iii

This is the last scene of this Act, located within the palace. Rosalind is deeply in love—so engrossed in melancholy reflections that she can hardly speak to anyone. Celia is amazed:

> ...is it possible, on such a sudden, you should fall into so strong a linking with old Sir Rowland's youngest son?[6]

Rosalind gives an indirect answer at first, but a few lines later declares her love quite openly:

> Let me love him for that, and do you love him because I do.[7]

Such sudden and intense passions are not at all uncommon in literature. In this case, particularly, Shakespeare had the example of his source, Lodge's *Rosalynde* (*vide* Ch. 8, *infra* for more information). The hero Rosander and the heroine Rosalynde fall suddenly and violently in love. Comparing the two authors Sylvan Barnett remarks:

> Shakespeare assumes that beautiful young people fall in love for no apparent reason.[8]

Shakespeare is, in fact, following a well-known literary convention, as well as his source material. Later in another scene (Act III, sc. v, ll. 80-81, p. 61) he refers to the well-known example of love at first sight as presented by Marlowe in *Hero and Leander*. Such events may be improbable in real life, but are quite common in drama, or in any other genre of literature.

Duke Frederick enters and the very first words he says on entering are to banish Rosalind. This action or something like it had already been seen impending in the preceding scene. When Rosalind asks what she has done to deserve this he says: "Thou art thy father's daughter, there's enough" (l. 58, p. 19). Celia pleads for her but to no avail.

After he goes away Celia tells Rosalind that she will go with her wherever she goes. It is she who decides where they shall go. Rosalind is too overcome to think and Celia tells her that they shall go to the forest of Arden. Rosalind is still in a miserable mood. Celia once more shows herself to be sensible and resourceful. She suggests that they disguise themselves. Inspired by this, Rosalind says that she being the taller of the two, would disguise herself as a boy and take the name of Ganymede who is the cup-bearer of the great good Jupiter. Celia says she will call herself Aliena. They also decide to take Frederick's clown with them as he will be a good companion. Now, full of the spirit of adventure, they go off to prepare for the journey.

This scene, like the former one, is partly in prose and partly in verse. The two girls talk to each other in prose and then, with the entrance of Frederick Shakespeare changes to blank verse and the rest of the scene is in poetry, and ends, like the preceding scene, with a couplet that reflects the thoughts of the princesses.

The scene is linked to the preceding and the following ones in that Rosalind's love for the handsome Orlando had already been hinted at in the foregoing scene. Again, after the pronouncement of banishment, the scene looks forward to the life, pastoral and innocent, in the forest of Arden in which this love will blossom forth.

The most important event of this scene is the angry rejection of Rosalind by her uncle. This had been foreshadowed in the preceding scene and thus forms a firm link with it. As a matter of fact three events occur in this scene: (a) Rosalind's confession of her love, (b) her banishment and (c) the two girls' decision to go to the forest in disguise. This second event is the only one that involves action. The first is a psychological state and the third also is a decision of the mind. The second event changes the whole life of Rosalind and Celia and provides the foundations for the rest of the play.

The scene can be divided into three distinct parts. The first part of the scene, in prose, comprises the dialogue between the cousins. Then a sinister element is introduced with the violence of Frederick after l. 38. This second part consists of the cruel banishment and lasts till Frederick leaves the stage. Then, with l. 90 the third part begins and the girls decide on their future course of action.

The scene takes the action forward in a firm and decided manner. The reader/audience is now prepared to be transported to the forest of Arden.

This is the last scene of this Act, one of the shortest in the play, comprising only three scenes. A lot of action is packed into it. The hero and heroine have fallen in love and the machinery for bringing them to the forest of Arden has been set in motion.

Act II, Scene i

Now the dramatist has brought us to the forest of Arden. The main events of the play will take place in this beautiful pastoral world far away from the evil and corruption of the court where treachery reigns supreme. It is a place that has been compared with other such places to which Shakespeare takes his characters, to tell of strange events:

> The forest of Arden ranks with the wood near Athens and Prospero's island, as a place set apart, even though, unlike them it is not ruled by magic.[9]

The Duke praises this life in the lap of Nature. It is a very important speech in which he points out that the forest presents its own hazards, but a man gains in knowledge and wisdom from them:

> And this our life, exempt from public haunt,
> Finds tongues in trees books in the running brooks,
> Sermons in stones and good in everything.[10]

Referring to these lines in particular Hazlitt exclaims:

> Never was there such beautiful moralizing, equally free from pedantry or petulance.[11]

They eat deer-meat or venison, this making Jaques, one of the courtiers, very melancholy. As a matter of fact Jaques is the typical "melancholy" man of Elizabethan plays and philosophizes over everything. The Duke wants to talk to him and with the prospect of this the scene ends.

The scene is entirely in verse and contains one of the most quoted passages in Shakespeare. The main function of the scene is to introduce the Duke and his followers, affording the reader a glimpse of the pastoral life they lead. It creates the mood of a willing acceptance of adversity as well as of peace and purity. It is a very short scene and serves to introduce the completely different kind of action to be presented from now on. It is not isolated from Act I, however, for the Duke's exile had been repeatedly mentioned earlier. It also looks forward to the future life of the Duke and the two girls.

Act II, Scene ii

This scene brings us back to the palace of Duke Frederick. It is a very short one and shows how the absence of the two princesses is discovered. Frederick is making enquiries about them and comes to know that his clown, too, is not to be found. The maid-servant of the princess also thinks that Orlando might have accompanied them. Frederick tells his men either to bring Orlando, or if he is absent, to get hold of Oliver.

This is a very short scene, of only 21 lines. It does not take the action forward, except to let the reader know that the flight of the two girls has been discovered. This, of course, was inevitable. It also makes the reader think that Orlando has also left for the forest, though as yet there is no reason why he should do so. The scene looks back to the last scene of Act I, in which the two girls had plotted their journey.

Act II, Scene iii

Now, after three scenes, the poet once more turns to Orlando. We had seen him last in Act I, sc. ii. Now we see him coming back home. Before he enters home Adam meets him in the adjacent grove and informs him that Oliver is out for his blood and tells him to keep away from the house, at any cost.

Orlando is bewildered and does not know what to do. He has no money and nowhere to go to. Adam has saved five hundred crowns and this he gives gladly to Orlando, asking him to take him along with him. Orlando is overwhelmed with gratitude and tells him that he will not be able to reward Adam for his help and sacrifice. The scene ends with their leaving the orchard together.

This scene is a very short one and, like the two preceding scenes, cannot be divided into parts. Like them, also, it is entirely in verse. The destination of Orlando and Adam is not mentioned. When they do come to the forest it seems that it is a matter of chance, and so it looks forward Act II, sc. iv, in which they reach the outskirts of the forest.

Act II, Scene iv

The real business of the play starts with this scene. Here Rosalind and Celia reach the outskirts of the forest and are absolutely tired out. Rosalind is in disguise as Ganymede and Celia as Aliena. They are accompanied by Touchstone.

They see Corin, an old shepherd, and Silvius, a young one, drawing near. Silvius is in love with a shepherdess, Phoebe, who scorns him. He is in despair and confides his troubles to Corin. Seeing his misery, Rosalind thinks of her own love for Orlando:

> Alas, poor shepherd! searching of thy wound
> I have by hard labour found my own.[12]

Touchstone tries to keep up their spirits by joking about his own love-affairs. Then they talk to Corin. Rosalind asks him to procure food for them and Corin tells them how he is employed by another man and how his master's cottage, flock of sheep and pasture ground are all for sale. At once Rosalind seizes this opportunity and offers to buy everything. She and Celia assure him that they will not only continue to employ him but also increase his wages.

Thus in this scene Rosalind and Celia are safely settled near the forest. It has been pointed out how, in order to enter this pastoral world of peace and love, the characters have to deserve it by undergoing some kind of suffering. Rosalind and Celia have both undergone the unaccustomed labour of journey by foot so that they reach the place absolutely at the end of their fortitude. They have also had to undergo mental suffering, for the former had been separated from her father and also banished from her home. Celia has had to renounce the comfortable life of a princess, and her inheritance, and disguise herself as a humble shepherdess. As we know she shall be rewarded later for her loyalty towards, and love for, Rosalind by gaining the love of Oliver, and presumably, living happily ever after.

The scene introduces conventional pastoral love. Silvius is the conventional rejected lover—a figure that recurs again and again in pastoral poetry. Many critics think that Shakespeare is mocking or parodying the artificiality of pastoral love through him. It has also been pointed out that Shakespeare has presented many different kinds of love in the play. Silvius's pastoral love is different from the courtly love of Orlando for Rosalind.

The scene is written in a mixture of prose and verse, Touchstone always speaking in prose. It ends, as is usual, with a Senecan couplet by Corin, which sums up his attitude to the two disguised girls:

> I will your very faithful feeder be,
> And buy it with your gold right suddenly.[13]

The scene is firmly linked to the foregoing scene in Act I in which Rosalind is banished. It is also linked to the later ones because now that they are safely established near the forest the ground is prepared for the later scenes in which Orlando and Rosalind will meet and have their game of love.

It is not a long scene, having only 97 lines, but can be divided into three distinct parts. The first is the prose conversation between the girls, with Touchstone's comments, till line 19. The second part consists of the dialogue between Corin and Silvius, from line 20 to 42. The rest of the scene makes up the third part. This is the most important part of the scene because here the immediate future of Rosalind and Celia is decided. This is the main event of the scene and therefore constitutes half of the entire scene.

It is noticeable that Corin does not suspect that Rosalind is a girl in disguise. He takes her to be a young man, addressing her as "gentle sir", "fair sir", etc. This is the case with all disguised characters. When Portia is disguised as a lawyer in *The Merchant of Venice* Bassanio does not know her. When Edgar is disguised in *King Lear* his own father does not recognise him. Impenetrability of disguise is a well-known feature of Elizabethan drama. A character might even put on just a different hat and mantle to disguise himself, and no one will recognise him. This is what has happened here. When, in a later scene she meets Orlando, even the keen eyes of a lover cannot at all pierce this impenetrability.

This disguise adopted by the two princesses will be kept till the very end of the play. It will be only in the last scene that the two of them will enter the stage as themselves. No other character except Viola in *Twelfth Night* dons a male disguise for so long a time. The Elizabethan custom of using young boys for female parts had made all this convenient.

Act II, Scene v

The scene opens with the famous song "Under the greenwood tree." This is the first song in the play and is sung by Amiens. It gives, to perfection, the aura of carefree life in the lap of nature. He sings one stanza and then Jaques importunes with him to sing another. After a few minutes Amiens sings the second stanza and then Jaques sings the reply. Amiens talk of a life that will be welcomed by all those who are not ambitious, and idealizes pastoral life as one of simple pleasure and contentment. Jaques gives the opposite view—the view of a worldly and very cynical man. According to him a man who has obstinately chosen a life in the forest is a fool:

> If it do come to pass
> That any man turn ass...
> Leaving his wealth and ease,
> A stubborn will to please.[14]

He uses a nonsense-word "ducdame" about which critics have given different opinions concerning the meaning. Jaques calls it an invocation to fools. The scene ends here, with preparations for a banquet for the Duke, whom Amiens goes to call.

It is a short scene with only 61 lines, and is noticeable for giving us the first two songs in the play. The dialogue is entirely in prose and does not take the action forward. No important events take place in it. Its main function is to create the pastoral atmosphere which it does far more effectively than the Duke's speech in the first scene of this Act. It highlights the pleasures of the forest and of unhurried contentment. The Duke is not present in this scene but even in his absence the lords who have come with him do not show any discontent.

The lords prepare a feast for the Duke while the song is going on and this is the meal that Orlando will interrupt in the seventh scene. So this scene is linked to the later one. Besides this, the scene introduces Jaques about whom there had been some talk in the first scene. It is thus linked to this former scene. Shakespeare takes pains even over a scene in which no events of importance take place, in order to integrate it within the structure of the play.

Act II, Scene vi

Now we come to one of the shortest of the scenes. Orlando and Adam are approaching the forest. Both of them are hungry but Adam being old is so debilitated that he cannot walk any further. He tells Orlando, with true love and self-sacrifice to abandon him and go forward. He prepares himself to die.

This, however, goes against Orlando's nature which is truly noble and affectionate. Instead of abandoning Adam he tries to breathe new heart into him and makes him sit leaning against a tree. He says he will go in search of food. Then, realising that leaving Adam alone in the open will not do, he takes Adam up in his arms and decides to put him in some kind of shelter. So, carrying him, Orlando goes out and the scene ends.

The scene contains only nineteen lines and is the second shortest scene of the play. It is written in prose and no events of importance happen in it. It does take the action forward in that Orlando has now been brought to the forest. Yet it has been tightly woven within the fabric of the play, for it is linked with the former scene in which Adam decides to accompany Orlando when he leaves his home. It is also connected to the next scene in which Orlando will interrupt the Duke's feast.

Though no important events occur in it, yet the scene is important in that it reveals Orlando's character. He had complained in the first scene that he had not been given the upbringing proper to a nobleman's son but here he is shown to have that inborn nobility which is his true heritage and does not depend upon any training or education. Old Adam is resigned to his fate, he knows that when servants like him grow old they are useless to their masters and therefore are neglected:

When service should in my old limbs lie lame.
And unregarded age in corners thrown.[15]

But Orlando does not do anything of the kind. He takes Adam in his arms, though he too is tired and hungry. He could not have done more if Adam had been his father. He shows that he is not just a romantic hero, capable only of courtly love, but a worthy young man who is capable of shouldering responsibilities. A new dimension is added to his character and he becomes worthy of our respect.

Act II, Scene vii

This is the last scene of this Act. The Duke has sat down to a repast with his lords. He wants to speak to Jaques, and Jaques appears with a smiling face. He has met Touchstone and, after having talked to him, wants to become a jester:

O that I were a fool!
I am ambitious for a motley coat.[16]

When the Duke says he shall have his heart's wish he praises fools in a long and important speech, specially the freedom fools have to speak their mind:

Invest me in my motley; give me leave
To speak my mind and I will through and through
Clean the foul body of th'infected world.[17]

He is interrupted by Orlando who enters with a drawn sword in his hand. As first he speaks very violently and demands food but when the Duke welcomes him in a gentle manner he calms down and tells him about himself and Adam. Then he goes out to fetch Adam and Jaques gives the set piece, the famous Seven Ages of Man speech.

This is one of the best-known passages of our poet and has been extensively anthologised and commented upon. Such set pieces stand a little apart from the rest of the dialogue and are, for the most time, of a meditative, philosophical kind. It is not that it is in elevated style but by nature such passages are serious and reward scrutiny.

After this Orlando returns with Adam and while they are all eating the Duke requests Amiens to sing. We now have the third song in the play, "Blow blow thou winter wind." While the song is being sung Orlando tells the Duke that he is Sir Rowland's son. The Duke welcomes him and Adam to join his retinue and the scene comes to an end.

This scene is entirely in verse and contains some of the most famous passages in Shakespeare. Besides these it also contains a song. As is customary the last two lines of the scene form a couplet.

The scene is directly linked to the fifth scene in which the feast is prepared. Here we see the Duke sitting down to eat. It is also linked to the sixth scene, immediately preceding it, in which Orlando and Adam reach the forest. He had set out to get food in that scene and here we see him coming to the feast. Also, by showing him join the Duke's group it prepares us to see him dwelling in the forest, so that he may, in due course of time, meet Rosalind.

It can be divided into three sections. The first part lasts till the entrance of Orlando. Three long speeches occur here. The first of them is narrative in nature but the next two ("It is my only suit" and "Why, who cries out on pride") are reflective ones. Then Orlando comes and the second part lasts till he goes out. Some time has to pass to allow him to go back to Adam and carry him to the Duke's feast. This problem is taken care of by Jaques's celebrated passage "All the world's a stage." Some critics might include this speech in the second part. Then Orlando enters carrying Adam. Here the third part begins. This third part may include Jaques speech or not, it is a matter of opinion. The speech is necessary from the point of view of stage-craft as a few minutes have to be given for Orlando to fetch Adam.

The most important event in the scene is the arrival of Orlando and his inclusion in the Duke's party. This meeting of the two (the Duke and Orlando) is brought about by chance and not by intent. Rosalind and Celia had to come because they expressly wanted to meet the Duke yet they do not meet him till the very end of the play whereas Orlando who had set out quite aimlessly, meets him first.

This is the last scene of this Act and this, the second Act, is the longest in the play. It has the maximum number of scenes, no less than seven of them. In contrast the first Act contains only three. Many important events occur in this Act. Both Orlando and Rosalind have to leave their homes and come to the forest of Arden. So altogether five characters (for Orlando has Adam and Rosalind her two companions) have, as of now, converged on the forest. This Act has also introduced the Duke's party and the two real pastoral characters, Corin and Silvius. Now all the main characters and most of the minor ones have been introduced. Shakespeare has, in a series of short scenes, finished the work of preparing for bringing the characters to the forest and also of creating the ideal pastoral atmosphere. In the next Acts, the stress will fall on the theme of love, some aspects of which will be developed in the next scene.

Act III, Scene i

This is the shortest scene in the play, comprising only eighteen lines. We are once more back at the Duke's palace. Oliver has been brought to Duke Frederick and he has said that his brother is missing. Frederick, getting very angry, confiscates his land and property and turns him out of doors, telling him that he must bring his brother within a year if he wants his property back.

This brief scene, entirely in verse, is linked to the scene (Act II, sc. ii.) in which Duke Frederick discovered the flight of the princesses and sent men to catch Orlando. It is also linked to the third scene of the next Act in which Oliver comes to Rosalind and tells her how he had reached the forest and all that happened thereafter. All the characters have to come to the forest and this scene serves the purpose of starting Oliver on his way to Arden. It also shows Frederick up as a malicious tyrant.

Act III, Scene ii

This is the longest scene of the play, containing 423 lines. It begins with love-lorn Orlando writing verses to Rosalind and hanging them on branches of trees, like the traditional lovers of romances. He then leaves the stage and Corin and Touchstone enter.

There follows a dialogue between the two of them in which a courtier's life is contrasted with a shepherd's life. Touchstone upholds the former and Corin the latter. After some time Rosalind enters and sees the paper with Orlando's poem on it and reads it aloud. It is a passage professing Orlando's fervent love for her and Touchstone, in mockery, instantly gives a parody of it. Then Celia comes with another page of Orlando's verses. The two girls talk about this odd phenomenon. Celia has already seen and talked to Orlando but, in the fashion of a young girl, she does not tell Rosalind this without teasing her a little at first. Even while they are talking Orlando and Jaques are seen coming towards them and they quickly hide behind a tree. From here they can see and hear Orlando, while themselves remaining invisible.

Jaques is teasing Orlando about Rosalind and after some time he goes away. Then Rosalind comes out from behind the tree and starts talking to him like, as she says, "a saucy lackey." It is a witty dialogue as indeed, all the dialogues in this scene are. Orlando is clearly captivated by this charming and witty young man. Rosalind tells him that there is someone in the forest who writes verses to someone called Rosalind and says that she would like to give some good advice to this man. Orlando confesses that he is this man. Rosalind says that love is a kind of madness and that she can cure it. Then comes the well-known proposal about the game of love: she will pretend to be Rosalind and Orlando will address her as such and treat her as such. Thus she will gradually cure him. He agrees:

Rosalind: I would cure you, if you would
but call me Rosalind and come
every day to my cote, and woo me.

Orl: Now by the faith of my love, I will.[18]

Then they all go off to the cottage in which Rosalind and Celia are staying and the scene ends.

The scene, the longest in the play, contains 423 lines and is written in a mixture of prose and verse. The dialogues are entirely in prose, but in the first part of the scene they are interspersed with the verses that Orlando has written and the parody by Touchstone. Of these verses the first is in quatrains. The second, which Rosalind reads aloud is in tetrametre couplets. The third, which Celia reads is again in quatrains. So, metrically, there is a lot of variety in this scene.

It is a long scene and can be divided into four parts. The first part is very short containing only Orlando's verses. The second part consists of the argument between Corin and Touchstone and lasts till the entrance of Rosalind. This continues till the entrance of Orlando and Jaques when the third part starts. This third part continues till the exit of Jaques and the entrance of Rosalind. So there is much coming and going of characters in this scene. Five characters drift in and out of it, yet there is no action as such. There is only dialogue.

The scene is linked in many ways to former scenes and the ensuing ones. It is one of the most important scenes in the play and occupies a key position. There are twenty-two scenes in the play and this is the twelfth, so it is almost the central scene of the play. It anticipates the future love-game between the hero and the heroine and also looks back to the second scene of Act I, for the hero and the heroine have been brought together after a gap of eight scenes, a full Act coming in between. Much has happened since then. Both of them have been forced to flee their home and take refuge in the wood. Even now they cannot really be said to be together as Orlando is not aware of Rosalind's identity. This dramatic irony will continue till the very end.

Act III, Scene iii

Another pair of lovers is brought in this scene—Touchstone and Audrey. So far there has been only one couple of lovers, Rosalind and Orlando. Though Silvius has been introduced, his beloved Phoebe was not. Here, however, the two lovers are together and make up another pair.

Touchstone is courting Audrey who is in a playful mood. Jaques comes in a little behind them and, unobserved, comments upon their talk. Touchstone proposes marriage and Audrey agrees. While they are talking the priest of the nearby village, Sir Oliver Martext, arrives. Touchstone seizes the opportunity of asking him to marry them then and there and Jaques offers to give away the bride. The marriage, however, does not take place for it is decided that the two of them will go to a church and there be properly married, not in this haphazard fashion.

Touchstone, in the happiness of his heart, sings a few lines and dances. This is the fourth song in the play and the scene ends with it.

The scene is entirely in prose, except for the song at the end. It serves the purpose of intensifying the love-interest by introducing a pair of humble lovers in contrast with the noble pair. It makes use of dramatic irony in that Jaques follows the lovers without their knowledge and delivers humorous comments. There is no malice in him, however, for he offers to expedite their marriage and gives good advice about it.

A new character is introduced here, Sir Oliver Martext. He is a very minor character and appears only in this scene, speaking only three sentences. It is an interesting feature of this play that new characters go on being introduced quite late into the play, till the very end. Three more characters still remain to be introduced and Sir Oliver is the least important of them.

Act III, Scene iv

Once more we see Rosalind and Celia talking. It is a humorous and witty dialogue, but the wit cannot hide Rosalind's intense love for Orlando. She also reveals how she had met the Duke her father but had not revealed her identity to him. There are many inconsistencies in the play and the fact that Rosalind lives near the forest and even meets her father while in disguise without revealing her identity is one of these improbabilities.

Meanwhile Corin comes and asks them to accompany him to where Silvius is sitting crying over his rejected love. The two cousins follow him and the scene ends.

The scene is in a mixture of prose and verse and serves the useful function of revealing the heroine's attitude. It also acquaints us with the fact that she has met her father. Though a short and unimportant scene it has been strongly and securely woven into the play by being firmly connected with the foregoing scene (the second in this Act) and the ensuing one, in which Rosalind, Celia and Corin meet Silvius and Phoebe.

Act III, Scene v

The third pair of lovers, Silvius and Phoebe, are introduced in this scene. They have been depicted as traditional pastoral lovers with the man loving and the maid disdainful. Silvius kneels and Phoebe is scornful. Rosalind, Celia and Corin enter from behind and observe them, unseen. They see that, in spite of Silvius's continued pleas, Phoebe goes on rejecting him. Then Rosalind advances and talks to her.

She is very severe and stern with Phoebe, telling her that this scorn does not become her, for she is in no way superior to him. Then she turns to Silvius and scourges him for pursuing a girl who insults him. She tells Phoebe that she fancies herself too much and should be thankful that, though she is nothing special yet Silvius loves her sincerely and wants to marry her:

> But mistress, know yourself—down on your knees
> And thank heaven, fasting, for a good man's love.[19]

The upshot is that Phoebe, taking her for a young and handsome boy, falls in love with her. As Rosalind-Ganymede goes away, Phoebe, longingly looking at her, gives the famous reference to Marlowe:

> Dead Shepherd, now I find thy saw of might,
> "Who ever loved, that loved not at first sight?"[20]

Rosalind-Ganymede's homily has had the effect of making her far gentler than she had been to Silvius. Then in a long speech she talks to him about Rosalind-Ganymede, disparaging her and says that she (Phoebe) will write a scornful letter to Ganymede and asks Silvius to deliver it. Silvius agrees, never dreaming that she is only deceiving him, having fallen in love with Rosalind.

The scene is in verse and adds to the romantic interest by introducing a third pair of lovers. It looks back to the foregoing scene in which Corin came and asked Rosalind and Celia to accompany him. It also looks forward to Act IV, sc. iii in which Silvius takes Phoebe's love-letter to Rosalind. It is the last scene of this Act.

The third Act of such plays is usually one in which the action starts to get complicated and that is what has happened here. Nearly all of the characters have been brought to the forest, the hero and the heroine have met (though in Orlando's case it is an indirect meeting) and two other pairs of lovers have been introduced. Already a love-triangle has been formed with Silvius, Phoebe and Rosalind-Ganymede. The dramatist will have to unravel all these complexities in the rest of the play.

Act IV, Scene i

In this scene, at last, there is a depiction of the love-game of Rosalind and Orlando. At first Rosalind and Celia are shown talking to Jaques. After some time Orlando comes. Rosalind at first pretends she has not seen him and then turns to him and chides him for being late. As had been decided in Act III, sc. ii, she is here pretending that she's Rosalind and Orlando has to greet her as such. There is a very complicated piece of irony here, for she is actually Rosalind, which Orlando does not know, and she is pretending to be Rosalind.

It is a long dialogue, very witty. Celia, though she is present on the stage, scarcely speaks. There is a mock-marriage sequence in which they pretend that Celia is the priest, marrying Rosalind to Orlando. The scene between them goes on for some more time and then Orlando goes away to attend the Duke. He promises that he will come after two hours. After he goes away Rosalind gives the strongest avowal of her love so far:

> ...my pretty little coz, that thou didst know how many fathoms deep I am in love! But it cannot be sounded.[21]

This scene is entirely in prose and presents the love-game of the aristocratic pair for the first time. It is, thus, linked to the second scene of the third Act. As Orlando is going to come back in two hours, it looks forward to the next scene also.

It is not that any important event occurs in this scene, but the love-game is an event itself. It is a charming and witty dialogue with a truly unprecedented element of dramatic irony. This dramatic irony occurs on three levels because the Elizabethan theatre used young boys to play the role of female characters. So the audience knows that there is, first of all, the boy actor who is pretending to be the heroine Rosalind. Rosalind is herself dressed as the boy Ganymede and, thirdly, for Orlando, Ganymede is pretending to be Rosalind. Thus here we have four distinct personalities in one—the boy actor, Rosalind, Ganymede and Rosalind again. It is a unique example of dramatic irony.

It can be divided into three distinct parts. The first section consists of the dialogue between Jaques and Rosalind, till line 30. Then the talk between Orlando and Rosalind makes up the second section, from line 31 to 195. The third section, starting with the exit of Orlando and lasting till the end, is the shortest of them.

There are not many scenes like this, where a love-scene is impeded by the disguise of the heroine. The nearest comparable scene is in *Twelfth Night* where Viola, in disguise tells Orsino indirectly of her love for him. Orsino is as unaware of the identity of Viola as Orlando is of that of Rosalind. The difference is that the scene in *Twelfth Night* is a serious one whereas this is a sportive scene, but the undercurrent of serious love is common to both.

It is noticeable that Celia is present throughout the scene, though she hardly speaks. Shakespeare observes the contemporary rules of decorum by not leaving the lovers alone. The scene is very far from being an ordinary love-scene, but it leaves the impression of strong and enduring love.

Act IV, Scene ii

This is one of the shortest scenes in the play, comprising only ten lines of dialogue and ten lines of song. The Duke's men have killed a deer and they bring it in triumphantly. The lord who has killed the deer is crowned with its horns and carried on the shoulders of the others. They sing the triumph-song of hunting, march three times around the tree and go into the cave.

The dialogue is so brief that it will take a very short time on the stage, but the scene has been prolonged by the song. The refrain is of six lines and is sung thrice. This scene is not so well integrated with the other scenes as we expect, but it provides the element of spectacle and music, both of which are essential elements of a play as given by Aristotle.

Though very short the scene can still be divided into two parts. The first part consists of the brief dialogue in the beginning and the second made up of the song and marching round the tree.

Act IV, Scene iii

In this scene Shakespeare takes us to Rosalind's cottage. By this time it is two in the afternoon and Rosalind is impatient at Orlando's failure to arrive. While they are waiting Silvius comes to them bringing Phoebe's letter, linking the scene thus with the fifth scene of the third Act. Phoebe's letter is actually a love-letter but Silvius has no notion of its being as such. Celia pities the poor man but Rosalind tries to rouse his self-respect. This is of no use, for Silvius is truly besotted and seeing this Rosalind sends him off with the message that if Phoebe wants Ganymede to love her then she in turn must love Silvius.

As Silvius goes away, Oliver comes. He is a man totally different from what he was before. At that time he was the lord of extensive estates and a cruel, avaricious and jealous brother. But all his property has been confiscated by Duke Frederick and he is a pitiable figure now. Again, at that time he hated Orlando but now he has undergone a sudden and total change of heart. He is a new man, both psychologically and materially. He tells the two girls his identity and how Orlando has saved his life by fighting a lioness. Now he himself is wounded and has sent his blood-stained handkerchief to Rosalind to tell her why he had not been able to keep his appointment with her.

Rosalind faints on hearing the story and on seeing the handkerchief. She recovers quickly and as it is unbecoming for a man to faint at the sight of blood, she tells Oliver that she had been pretending. Oliver goes with them into the cottage and the scene ends.

The scene is in a mixture of prose and verse. Besides the blank verse of dialogue there is also the verse-letter from Phoebe which is in octosyllabic couplets. It is linked to the fifth scene of the third Act because Phoebe had said in it that she will send Rosalind-Ganymede a letter. This is the letter that Silvius brings. Also, in Act IV, sc. i, Orlando had promised to come back at two o'clock and here Rosalind is waiting for him. It also looks forward to Act V, sc. ii in which Rosalind and Orlando meet and Phoebe receives her answer from Silvius.

Now the last of the characters who had to be brought to the forest from the outside world, Oliver, has been brought in. He and Celia are going to make up the fourth pair of lovers, though as yet no indication of this has been given. The most important event of the scene is the arrival and conversion of Oliver.

This is the last scene of Act IV and the dramatist is already gathering the strands of the plot in order to bring about a neat and happy conclusion. This Act has heightened the love-interest by showing the love-game and also by making Phoebe fall in love with Rosalind-Ganymede. It shows the conversion of Oliver as well.

Act V, Scene i

This is one of those scenes that are concerned only with the characters of the sub-plot. Touchstone and Audrey are talking about their marriage. Then another new character is brought in, William, the rejected lover of Audrey. He is put through a regular catechism by Touchstone who asks him his name, his age, his means, etc. He demoralizes William thoroughly and drives him off. Then Corin comes and tells them they are wanted by Rosalind and Celia. They follow him.

This scene is unimportant and very much like padding put in to lengthen out the fifth Act. The new character William helps create the second love-triangle in the play. Thus, there are now two love-triangles, Rosalind-Orlando-Phoebe, and Touchstone-Audrey-William. Thus, though unimportant and easily omittable, yet this scene is not entirely irrelevant and the former courting scene (Act III, sc. iii) links it with the main plot. It is entirely in prose.

Act V, Scene ii

This scene shows Orlando and Oliver talking and through their talk it becomes clear that Oliver and Celia are in love and have become engaged. Orlando is surprised at the speed at which this has been accomplished. Oliver tells him that these things are beyond reason. He has decided that after marriage he and Aliena will stay here and lead a pastoral life. All the property he has inherited from his father will now devolve upon Orlando, though actually it is in Frederick's grip.

Orlando agrees gladly and it is decided that the marriage will take place the next day. Then Oliver goes away to prepare Celia for this sudden wedding, and Rosalind comes in. They talk about the whirlwind courtship of Oliver and Celia. Rosalind describes it:

> your brother and my sister no sooner met but they looked, no sooner looked but they loved; no sooner loved but they sighed; no sooner sighed but they asked one another the reason; no sooner knew the reason but they sought the remedy: and in these degrees have they made a pair of stairs to marriage.[22]

Orlando is sad at the thought that his brother will get married to the woman of his choice but he himself will never be able to do so. Rosalind then tells him that she has a learned magician for her uncle and can do strange things. She assures him that when Oliver marries Aliena the next day he too shall marry Rosalind.

Silvius and Phoebe then enter the stage and there is an entertaining dialogue in which each professes his or her love: Orlando for his Rosalind, Silvius for Phoebe and Phoebe for Ganymede. Rosalind herself repeats but one sentence every time: "And I for no woman." The dialogue goes like this:

Phoebe: Good shepherd, tell this youth what 'tis to love,

Silvius: It is to be all made of sighs and tears,
And so am I for Phoebe.

Phoebe: And I for Ganymede.

Orlando: And I for Rosalind.

Rosalind: And I for no woman.[23]

The dialogue goes on like this for twenty lines more. Finally, Rosalind gets tired of bandying words and calls for an end to it.

She then tells all of them that she will help them get their heart's desire the next day and asks them all to meet her the next morning.

The scene is in a mixture of prose and verse. Orlando, Oliver and Rosalind talk in prose in the beginning and verse is used when the two, shepherd and shepherdess, enter. At first this dialogue is in ordinary blank verse and then from line 80 (quoted above) onwards it develops into a very stylized poetry with continuous stichomythia (*vide* Ch. 10, *infra*). After that when Rosalind addresses all of them she does so in prose.

The scene is linked to the foregoing scene in that it repeatedly refers to Act IV, sc. iii in which Oliver had met Celia and Rosalind had read the letter sent by Phoebe. It also looks forward to the next scene in that Rosalind refers again and again to the next day. Indeed the next day is going to be a crucial one, for Oliver is to marry Celia and Rosalind has promised Orlando that he shall marry her. She has also promised Silvius that he too shall get married on the morrow and so shall she herself.

The scene is divisible into three distinct parts. The first part consists of the short prose dialogue between Orlando and Oliver and the second of the longer dialogue between Orlando and Rosalind (Lines 19-71). The last part of the scene commences with the entrance of Silvius and Phoebe and ends with Rosalind's exhortation to each of them to meet her on the morrow.

It is a scene which with its continuous reference to the next day strongly gives an impression that the end of the play is drawing near. Yet the next scene is not the last. The actual end of the play is postponed by the intervention of another scene.

Act V, Scene iii

This scene, like the first one of this Act, is in the nature of a fillip. Nothing of note happens in it Touchstone and Audrey are happy that they shall marry the next day. Then two of the Duke's pages come up and sing a duet that creates the atmosphere of the tender love of spring-time. It is one of the best songs in this play, though it is said to be a 'foolish song' by Touchstone.

Act V, Scene iv

This is the last scene of the play. All the main characters except Rosalind are already there on the stage and after a very brief dialogue between Orlando and the Duke, Rosalind enters, along with Silvius and Phoebe. Rosalind asks the Duke if he is ready to give Rosalind in marriage to Orlando and the Duke agrees and so does Orlando. Then she asks Phoebe whether she is ready to marry Silvius if she refuses to marry Ganymede and Phoebe as well as Silvius agree. She then leaves the stage and so also does Celia.

Now some time has to be given for the actors to change their dresses, and there is a long and witty dialogue in prose between Jaques and Touchstone. This dialogue is not necessary for the play but it is essential from the point of view of stagecraft. Changing from a male shepherd-boy to the female dress of a princess is no easy matter and quite a few minutes have to be provided for.

Then there follows a masque (*vide* Ch. 8, *infra* for an explanation of this term) in which Hymen the god of marriage comes in with Rosalind and Celia and his retinue. The two princesses are no longer in disguise. There is, first of all, a song by Hymen in which he gives Rosalind to the Duke:

> Good duke, receive thy daughter,
> Hymen from Heaven brought her,
> Yea, brought her hither,
> That thou mightst join her hand with his
> Whose heart within her bosom is.[24]

The song then stops for a little time while Rosalind, the Duke, Orlando and Phoebe talk. It is a brief but pithy dialogue. The Duke accepts Rosalind as his daughter, Orlando recognizes her as his beloved and Phoebe realizes that Ganymede is a woman.

Hymen then resumes his song, saying that there are eight young men and women who must join their hands in his presence. He addresses each pair and blesses them. Then a choric song celebrating the marriage, is sung, praising Juno the goddess of marriage, and Hymen.

An important event takes place after this. A completely new character, Jaques de Boys, who is the second son of Sir Rowland de Boys and thus the elder brother of Orlando (Oliver being the eldest) comes in. He introduces himself and tells the assembled company that while Duke Frederick was coming to the forest with an army to kill the exiled Duke, he met a holy man and was converted. Now he has renounced the world and has returned his kingdom to Duke Senior.

The Duke hears the news of his reinstatement with equanimity. The celebrations are continued with redoubled vigour. Before the singing and dancing commence, however, Jaques (the melancholy man who is the follower of the Duke) holds up the proceedings for a few minutes. He declares that he will not go back to the court but, like the newly converted Frederick, adopt the life of a hermit.

This, the final scene of the play, contains great variety in the way of versification. It is written in a mixture of prose and verse. It begins with a verse dialogue which lasts till the entrance of Touchstone and Audrey. The long dialogue between Jaques and Touchstone is in prose. Then with the entrance of Hymen and others verse predominates. The dialogues are in blank verse interspersed with Hymen's song. The last few lines spoken by the Duke and Jaques are in couplets. So much variety is but rare in just one scene.

The scene can be divided into four parts. The first part, in blank verse, comes to an end as Touchstone and Audrey enter following the exit of the two princesses. The second part consists of the prose dialogue between Touchstone and Jaques. Then the third part commences with the entrance of Hymen and the others and lasts till Phoebe's acceptance of Silvius. Then the last part begins with the entrance of Jaques de Boys.

As the last scene of a romantic comedy it is ideal. All the characters except Frederick are present on the stage and there are no less than four happy marriages. There is reconciliation between Oliver and Orlando. The Duke's kingdom is restored to him and Orlando also gets his inheritance. Everyone looks forward to a happy and prosperous future. This is symbolized by the dance at the end.

The Epilogue

Though Shakespeare has not given any Prologue to the play, he has given it an Epilogue. This comes right at the end and is spoken by Rosalind. It is a witty passage in prose. In it she exhorts the audience to accept and enjoy the play as the light-hearted entertainment it is meant to be:

> I charge you, O women, for the love that you bear to men, to like as much of this play as please: and I charge you, O men, for the love you bear to women—as I perceive by your simpering, none of you hates them—that between you and the women the play may please.[25]

As can be seen, the title of the play has also been worked into this speech: "to like as much of this play as may please." It is written in the traditional manner, asking the audience to like and applaud the play. The only unusual feature is the fact that it is delivered by a female character. It is, in all, a most appropriate end to a romantic comedy.

REFERENCES

1. Act I, sc. i, ll 17-19, p. 3
2. Act I, sc. i, ll. 154-59, pp. 7-8.
3. Act I, sc. i, ll. 110-13, p. 6.
4. Act I, sc. ii, ll. 245-46, p. 16.
5. Act I, sc. ii, ll. 250-53, p. 16.
6. Act I, sc. iii, ll. 26-28, p. 18.
7. Act I, sc. iii, ll. 36-37, p. 18.
8. Barnett, Sylvan, *Strange Events: Improbability in As You Like It*, in Brown, J.R., *op. cit.*, p. 176.
9. Gardner, Helen, *op. cit.*, p. 157.
10. Act II, sc. i, ll. 15-17, p. 22.
11. Brown, John Russell, *op. cit.*, p. 33.
12. Act II, sc. iv, ll. 43-45, p. 29.
13. Act II, sc. iv, ll. 96-97, p. 30.
14. Act II, sc. v, ll. 48-51, p. 32.
15. Act II, sc. iii, ll. 41-42, p. 26.
16. Act II, sc. vii, ll. 42-43, p. 35.
17. Act II, sc. vii, ll. 58-60, p. 35.

18. Act III, sc. ii, ll. 415-17, p. 53.
19. Act III, sc. v, ll. 57-58, p. 61.
20. Act III, sc. v, ll. 81-82, p. 61.
21. Act IV, sc. i, ll. 200-02, p. 69.
22. Act V, sc. ii, ll. 31-36, p. 80.
23. Act V, sc. ii, ll. 79-84, p. 81.
24. Act V, sc. iii, ll. 108-12, p. 88.
25. The Epilogue, ll. 11-16, p. 92.

5

The Major Themes

A definite central theme gives unity to any work. It is, therefore, desirable that a play should have a certain theme, or idea, or contents, on which it can be based. It is one of the greatest difficulties that any student of Shakespeare has to face that the manifold complexities of his plays baffle the reader so much that it becomes difficult to determine what the theme of a certain play is. *As You Like It* is classified as a romantic comedy and the theme of such a play is love and marriage. All the romantic comedies of Shakespeare fulfill this requirement and end with multiple unions. There are four marriages in the present play. It would, therefore, seem that love is the supreme theme here. This itself has been looked at from many different angles and, in addition, many critics have thought of other themes as well. Even they later, however, conceded that love is the undisputed central theme.

This theme is so clear that it hardly needs to be explained. All the same, in contrast with the other play, this theme is at times eclipsed by the theme of pastoralism. In addition, there are certain sub-themes like those of betrayal, courtly life versus pastoral life, etc. Let us first see what treatment the theme of love has received in his hands.

(A) THE THEME OF LOVE

The importance of love as a theme in romantic comedies and the Elizabethan attitude to it has already been discussed (*vide* Ch. 3, *supra*). Critics, in their own ways, have given different accounts of this all-important theme.

The theme of love, according to P.G. Phialas, is present in three different ways: (a) "The rejection of love by persons who later succumb to it", (b) "sentimental idealization of it", and (c) a realistic view of it."[1] All of these are to be found in the play before us. Phoebe rejects Silvius's love at first and then succumbs to the misleading charms of Rosalind-Ganymede. Audrey, too, had rejected William but then succumbs to Touchstone. Silvius as well as Orlando idealize love. Thus, in the play romantic love and pastoral love run side by side. Touchstone represents the realistic view. Rosalind provides a balance between them. She is "many fathoms deep in love", yet in her advice to Phoebe she is very practical, telling her to sell while she can for she is not for all markets. She laughs at Orlando and berates Silvius for running after Phoebe yet it is she who tells Phoebe: "Thank heaven, fasting, for a good man's love."

It is in his treatment of romantic love that Shakespeare shows a definite departure from his source. In Lodge, there is both romantic love and pastoral love but he does not relate the two. It was Shakespeare who had the imagination and the capacity to bring the two together, and thus achieve perfect harmony:

> It qualifies both the Petrarchan hyperboles of romantic lovers like Orlando and the exclusively physical concept of anti-romantic characters like Touchstone.[2]

It is also noticeable that Shakespeare presents the success and the validity of all of these attitudes by showing all of these widely different couples united by marriage. Phoebe's love for Rosalind-Ganymede proves to be a mirage and she is united to the lover she had rejected. Audrey, however, does succumb to a person different from the one she had rejected. Oliver and Celia love each other in the conventional manner and are united. Rosalind who harmonizes the different attitudes to love, gives herself to the romantic lover, Orlando.

John Dover Wilson gives more or less the same three diversions, but his treatment is different. Shakespeare, he says, takes the conventional lovers from Lodge—the scornful Phoebe and the mournful Silvius and uses them to show-up in contrast the genuine passions of Rosalind and Orlando. The third type of love is provided by Audrey and Touchstone. Again, he finds that there is further contrast between the ideal shepherd and shepherdess (Silvius-Phoebe) and the genuine country bumpkins (William and Audrey). All these pairs of lovers are compared and contrasted and played against each other. Different types of love are not just portrayed but compared with each other. From this point of view *As You Like It* is a more complex play than his other comedies.

It has also been said that Shakespeare has gradually brought about a maturer comprehension of the nature of love in his comedies and this reaches its climactic achievement in this play.

> In Rosalind and Orlando of *As You Like It* the dramatist again depends upon a growth in the comprehension of love which subsequently leads them to a fuller realization of their true personalities.[3]

Thus, Orlando is at first a rebellious younger brother, chafing against the tyranny of his elder brother. Then love comes into his life. He has to flee the court, and then his home and finally has to take refuge in the forest. Here he has respite from the cruelties of fate and develops into the typical Petrarchan lover. Then he meets Rosalind in disguise and she proceeds to cure him of his idealism and sentimentalism. Then, as he comes to know of the seriousness of Oliver's love that is going to lead to marriage the next day, he realizes that the game of love he has been playing all these days with Rosalind-Ganymede is not enough, and he confesses this to Rosalind:

> Orlando: By so much the more shall I tomorrow be at the height of heart-heaviness, by how much I shall think my brother happy in having what he wishes for.
>
> Ros.: Why then, tomorrow I cannot serve your turn for Rosalind?
>
> Orl.: I can live no longer by thinking.[4]

There is only this one brief sentence but it makes Rosalind realize that Orlando's love has now left the earlier impractical idealization behind and is ready for mature responsibilities and she decides to reveal her identity on the morrow.

Not only this, but, being in love brings about maturity in Orlando in other respects as well. He is able not only to gain the nobility of forgiving his elder brother but even to save his life. Love has brought about great development in his nature:

> Obviously then, through the catalyst of Love, Orlando's personality is purged and his highest qualities realized.[5]

Rosalind's personality also undergoes a like development. Right in the beginning she had hesitatingly admitted that she was in love. She had been proud and this pride had been humbled: "my pride fell with my fortune" (Act I, sc. i, l. 240, p. 15). Later when she meets Orlando she cannot bring herself to reveal her identity to him and plays the game of love in disguise. Here also, only through a playful irony does she profess to cure him by schooling him. But then she observes Phoebe's attitude to Silvius and realizes how much suffering female pride or vanity can inflict upon a lover. Her advice to Phoebe to thank heaven fasting for a good man's love makes her own attitude clear and she can finally give herself to Orlando.

The theory of green world comedy (*vide* Ch. 3, *supra*) presents its own interpretation concerning the treatment of love in such plays. The closed-world comedies (*The Merchant of Venice, Twelfth Night,* etc.) with which the green world comedies are contrasted give a less romantic treatment of love than the latter do. There is the element of conflict or some kind of discord in the former and this element also exists in green world comedies. But here the conflicts are not as serious as in the others:

> *As You Like It* suggests by its little that the dramatic conflict within the forest of Arden is a dialectic conflict of tastes and attitudes.[6]

Thus, Orlando's attitude of a Petrarchan lover is ridiculed by Rosalind who professes to cure him of this love by her schooling. All the conflicting ideas and attitudes have to be reconciled with love. As a matter of fact, the schooling she gives does make his love develop and ripen. Shakespeare, in a benign mood, has treated this love very indulgently:

> Orlando and Rosalind in the springtime of their passion are ourselves as wish we were.[7]

One important conflict in this green world is the gender conflict. The most important lesson that love teacher is to humble oneself and to give oneself in love and truthfulness and trust. This humility and trust cannot come so long as there is any kind of antagonism present. This is the reason why reconciliation and marriage are so important in comedy. Marriage negates antagonism and affirms the dramatist's faith in life. So different kinds of persons are brought together and joined in holy matrimony in this play—whether they are romantic lovers or pastoral or realistic ones.

(B) THE THEME OF PASTORALISM

As this play has been recognized from the very beginning as a pastoral play so the theme of ideal pastoralism is as important in it as of love. Critics have found many different treatments of this theme in the play. Some of them can be catalogued thus:

(a) The courtly romance of princesses playing at shepherds and shepherdesses (Rosalind and Celia);

(b) The pastoral eclogue of the rejected shepherd and the scornful shepherdess (Silvius and Phoebe);

(c) The parody of the above (Touchstone and Audrey); and

(d) The moral tradition of the wise shepherd (Corin).

The first of these, of course, is the main plot. Rosalind and Celia adopt the disguise of a shepherd and shepherdess out of prudence and necessity as they are travelling virtually by themselves, with only Touchstone for escort. So for reasons of safety they adopt the disguise. After they reach the forest they do not abandon the disguise. Instead they reinforce it by buying the property of a farmer and settle down to a pastoral life. This is for a short time only, but the very fact that they keep up this pretence at all proves that it fulfills a desire and a need deep in their hearts—the need for a simple and innocent life in the lap of nature. They abandon the disguise at the end of the play and it is also clear that they will be going back to court but even a short spell of this life will remain a treasured memory forever in their hearts. It is a recognized fact that the pastoral convention arose out of a desire for a simple, innocent and pure life. Real life is limited and unsatisfactory to say the least, and one wants to go back to the primal life of purity, to the Golden Age. William Empson has put it in a very succinct manner:

> in pastoral you take a limited life and pretend it is the full and normal one, and a suggestion that one must do this with all life because the normal is itself limited.[8]

This is exactly what Rosalind and Celia do, and after the golden days in the forest are over, they once more go back to normal life.

The second form of the pastoral (that of the rejected lover and the scornful shepherdess as found in the eclogues of the classical poets) is the most conventional and traditional one but the main persons are not concerned directly. It is found here in the courting of Phoebe by Silvius. His attitude and diction are exactly those to be found in traditional pastoral poem. Both of them behave according to expectation:

Sil: O dear Phoebe,
If ever—as that ever may be near—
You meet in some fresh cheek the power of fancy
Then shall you know the wounds invisible
That love's keen arrows make.

Ph.: But till that time
Come not near me: and when that time comes,
Afflict me with thy mocks, pity me not,
As till that time I shall not pity thee.[9]

It has been suggested that in this sub-plot Shakespeare has satirized the pastoral convention, that the play is:

> an exquisite essay in the pastoral manner and a sly criticism of it.[10]

Whether it is a criticism or not, this is definitely a variation on the theme of the pastoral in the play.

It has been suggested that this aspect of the pastoral theme has been parodied in the Touchstone and Audrey plot. Instead of genuine shepherds and shepherdesses we have a clown and a goat-girl. We have a realistic view of life in Touchstone as contrasted with the romantic one of Orlando. Though Audrey pretends to hold him off and never answers him directly whether she loves him or not the minute that Touchstone shows he is serious by mentioning the priest she, however indirectly, accepts him: "Well, the gods give us joy." She is no disdainful shepherdess like Phoebe and Touchstone is an entirely sensible down-to-earth man who has no illusions about love itself or his beloved:

> A poor virgin, sir, an ill-favoured thing, sir, but mine own—a poor humour of mine, sir to take that that no man else will.[11]

There is no need, however, to regard this plot as a parody of the Silvius-Phoebe plot, for none of the characters is a shepherd. Touchstone is a court jester and Audrey a country girl. It can stand on its own. Helen Gardner, however, regards this play as a parody of the Silvius and Phoebe plot and so it can be considered as being pastoral by default. Though she does not analyse the plot from this point of view she clearly calls this sub-plot a burlesque of Silvius's wooing of Phoebe.[12]

The fourth aspect of the pastoral theme as listed above is to be found in the old shepherd Corin. He is the wise old shepherd of pastoral world. He is no sentimental romanticizer of the pastoral but a true shepherd who has to labour for his living. He tries to instill some sense into Silvius's fiery heart and also to console him:

> Cor.: That is the way to make her scorn you still.
>
> Sil.: O Corin, that thou knew'st how I do love her!
>
> Cor.: I partly guess: for I have loved ere now.[13]

Later, talking with Touchstone, he describes his own life and attitude as a shepherd:

> Sir, I am true labourer. I earn that I eat, get that I wear, owe no man hate, envy no man's happiness, glad of

> other men's good, content with my harm; and the greatest of my pride is to see my ewes graze and my lambs suck.[14]

This justly famous description gives all the innocent pleasures and simple ambitions of the simple and innocent life of a shepherd. Corin is not, like Touchstone, learned in the ways of the world but wisdom learnt through experience is far superior to any superficial knowledge.

These four varieties of the theme of simple pastoral life run throughout the play, each most effectively highlighting the others in contrast. As has been pointed out Shakespeare has united the twin themes of pastoralism and of love that Lodge, from whom he took his material, had failed to do:

> Shakespeare's purpose was not to reproduce a romantic tale laid in a pastoral scene with its conventional attributes but rather to express a significant relationship between romantic love and the pastoral conventions and to dramatize attitudes towards them.[15]

Only a few of the critical interpretations of the theme of pastoralism have been given above. There are many other interesting variations which enrich our understanding and appreciation.

(C) THE THEME OF PLAY

This is the view of D.J. Palmer. He thinks that *As You Like It* is a play with the minimum amount of the narrative element and the whole emphasis falls on the element of play. He says:

> The heart of the comedy might be described as a demonstration of man's natural propensity for play.[16]

He points out that right from the very beginning the forest of Arden is associated with the carefree attitude of mind that betokens sportiveness. Thus, when Charles the wrestler refers to it in the first scene he brings together the idea of legendary Merry England and that of the Golden Age:

> they live like the old Robin Hood of England. They say many young gentlemen flock to him every day and fleet the time carelessly, as they did in the Golden World.[17]

It seems life in the forest is like a pleasant pastime to the Duke and his followers.

Then after Rosalind is banished, the two girls are at first very naturally down-hearted. But soon they pick up their spirits and start to devise the ways and means of leaving the palace. It is as if they are planning for an entertainment—a fancy-dress party or something like it:

> A gallant curtle-axe upon my thigh,
> A boar-spear in my hand, and in my heart
> Lie there what hidden woman's fear there will,
> We'll have a swashing and a martial outside.[18]

When we see the Duke in the forest of Arden for the first time he is in a serious mood, advocating the pastoral life precisely for the moral upliftment it gives. But this too is like a game, says David Palmer:

> It is only the nature of the game that is different: this is just as much an exercise in make-belief as playing at Robin Hood.[19]

The Duke looks upon the obstacles presented by forest life as a moral lesson devised by a kind yet stern Nature. He is ready to make the best of things and it is this sweetness of temper, this ability to adjust that Amiens admires when he comments upon the Duke's speech.

Moreover, the Duke shows that he is able to appreciate the benevolence of nature as well as her cruelties in the spirit of a sportsman, for he proposes to go hunting, and this has always been regarded as a royal sport. This proposal brings to us the description of Jaques's moralizings over a wounded deer. The Duke is ready to find some matter for sport even in Jaques's attitude and says he shall talk to Jaques in a spirit of pure playfulness and tolerance.

Analysing this particular scene (Act II, sc. i) Palmer says that here we have an exposition of the highly equivocal nature of play. The same person can be the victim of misfortune as well as causing misfortune to others. The Duke had been a victim of treachery by his brother, but in the forest he is causing misery to the animals by hunting them. His kingdom had been usurped by his brother, but in the forest he is usurping the place of those who are native to it. In like manner, Jaques inveighs against the hunters who kill the deer and they, in their turn, make him the butt of their mockery. It is all in the game, a game whose paradigm goes on changing continuously:

> these games are a bitter-sweet mixture of whimsical sentiment and wanton cruelty.[20]

The entire play has been interpreted from this point of view. The love-game of Rosalind and Orlando naturally takes the pride of place in the discussion, though other incidents also do not go neglected, the discussion between Jaques and the jester before the end of the play "round off this comedy of pastimes."[21]

The more one studies the themes that are dealt with in Shakespeare's plays, the more complexities are to be founds. Henri Fluchère, indeed, is of the opinion that the themes make up the richness of the plays:

> The secret of Shakespeare's strange attraction, the presence of something that beggars all description and seems to be an instinctive knowledge of the roots of being whence the phenomena sprint, is to be looked for, no doubt, in the study of the themes.[22]

REFERENCES

1. Phialas, P.G., *op. cit.*, p. xiv.
2. *Ibid.*, p. 24.
3. Champion, L.S., The Evolution of Shakespeare's Comedy: A Study in Dramatic Perspective, Harvard University Press, 1973, p. 65.
4. Act V, sc. ii, ll. 43-48, p. 80.
5. Champion, *op. cit.*, p. 66.
6. Hawkins, Sherman, *op. cit.*, p. 61.
7. *Ibid.*, p. 62.
8. Empson, William, *Some Versions of the Pastoral*, London, 1935, pp. 114-15.
9. Act III, sc. v, ll. 27-34, p. 60.
10. Wilson, John Dover, *op. cit.*, p. 146.
11. Act V, sc. iv, ll. 57-59, p. 86.

12. Gardner, H., *op. cit.*, p. 149.
13. Act II, sc. iv, ll. 21-23, p. 28.
14. Act III, sc. ii, ll. 71-75, p. 43.
15. Phialas, P.G., *op. cit.*, p. 223.
16. Palmer, D.J., *As You Like It* and *the Idea of Play*, in Brown, *op. cit.*, p. 183.
17. Act I, sc. i, ll. 110-13, p. 6.
18. Act I, sc. iii, ll. 117-20, p. 21.
19. Palmer, *op. cit.*, p. 186.
20. *Ibid.*, p. 188.
21. *Ibid.*, p. 197.
22. Fluchère, Henri, *Shakespeare*, Longmans, Green and Co., London, 1953, p. 195.

6

The Major Characters

(A) SHAKESPEARE'S CHARACTERS

All the different features of Shakespeare's plays have enchanted serious readers, but the one that is perhaps the most productive of critical interpretation is that of characterization, Shakespeare truly has no rival here. Characters, specially those in drama, have to be lifelike, but Shakespeare's characters often go beyond mere realism, for they take on symbolic significance, thus gaining universality. Moreover, unlike many dramatists of his time, Shakespeare pays attention to his minor figures also. This adds significantly to the impression of rich crowded life in his plays.

He has given more portraits to the gallery of memorable characters than any other writers. Be it heroes, heroines, or villains, Shakespeare has a greater number and a richer variety than anyone else. We have the great tragic heroes Hamlet, King Lear *et al.*, the heroines like Rosalind, Miranda and others, as well as the no less great villains' like Iago, Shylock *et al.*

It has to be remembered, moreover, that he never reached a stagnation-point. As his art matured, so did his character-portrayal. He himself gained more and more insight into the complicities of the human mind, and his characters also became correspondingly more and more complex. To call his characters realistic does not seem to be enough. This was realized by Pope:

> His characters are so much Nature herself that 'tis a sort of injury to call them by so distant a name as copies of hen.[1]

As in all things, this inimitable art of being able to depict characters developed with time and the early works show evidences of immaturity. The characters of his early phase lack sharp individualization. The pairs of lovers in *A Midsummer Night's Dream* are barely distinguishable from each other and the witty lords and ladies of *Love's Labour's Lost* also merge into each other. The only character who really stands out in these early plays is Bottom in the former.

As the years of experimentation and of apprenticeship are left behind, the different characters come into sharper focus. We have the important male figures of the Chronicle plays and the heroines of the golden comedies. The lively heroines of these comedies, Rosalind in the play under discussion, Portia of *The Merchant of Venice*, Beatrice of *Much Ado About Nothing* and Viola of *Twelfth Night* gain so much importance that the heroes of these plays (Orlando, Bassanio, Benedick and Duke Orsino respectively) are pushed into the background. It is, paradoxically, a villain who is the only male character who towers above all the others—Shylock in *The Merchant of Venice*.

One has to wait till the third stage of his career before coming across the great male figures. The great tragedies and the problem comedies deal with the predominance of evil and suffering and here it is that one finds the titanic characters of tragic heroes. Hamlet, Othello, Lear and Macbeth all came into being during this time, and Lady Macbeth is an astounding female figure. It is with reference particularly to these that Pope's words seem to become significant (quoted above).

The last Romances produce a different kind of characters. Here the viewpoint has changed. It is no longer the problem of evil that concerns him, but man's reaction to it. The themes of sin leading to repentance which in its turn leads to purification become important. Now the dramatist shows his heroes undergoing a spiritual journey and after suffering prolonged remorse for the sins committed, he emerges a sadder and a wiser man. A younger, purer generation comes into being, to whom the future is handed over. These characters thus gain a symbolic significance, which takes them a step above universality.

These are the qualities that set Shakespeare's characters apart from those of the others. Yet these are not all, for it must be remembered that he did not create the characters out of thin air. Most of them were already present in the sources, he created but very few new characters. Moreover, he had to present his characters in conformity with the basic classical rules and contemporary conventions. This again, is another of his qualities that excite admiration:

> It is equally undeniable that, allowing for his own peculiar genius, he conforms with the accepted conventions of characters-drawing as with other conventions.[2]

Two kinds of guidelines were available to him (and to everyone else). First there were the rules laid down by Aristotle and expounded by later critics, particularly: those of Renaissance Italy. Practical examples were to be found in the classical plays he had read while in school (*vide* Ch. 2, Life and Works, *supra*), Seneca for tragedies, Plautus and Terence for comedies. In addition there were many other works that defined and gave examples of characters, written by his contemporaries. Some such books are: Newton's *The Touchstone of Complexions*, Bishop Hall's *Characters of Virtues and Vices*, Sir Thomas Overbury's *Characters,* etc. Any dramatist of the time could turn to these books when in need of a character for his play. All of them could, but there was only one Shakespeare. He wrought miracles with the same material everyone had.

The tradition of writing character-sketches goes back to Aristotle, as indeed, so many traditions do. In his *Nichomachaean Ethics* Aristotle had given elaborate descriptions of several different types of characters. By the time of the Renaissance, so many characters had been added to Aristotle's list that Theophrastus gave more than a hundred of them. These are what Quintilian had called "set definitions of fixed characters." These are all practical examples, but in *Poetics* Aristotle had laid down clear-cut rules for portraying dramatic character. There are four traits all characters should have (a) Proportion, (b) Appropriateness, (c) Realism, and (d) Consistency.

The quality of Proportion (also translated as Goodness), has a deeply moral implication. The intention underlying any action or speech must be good:

> Any speech or action that manifests moral purpose of any kind will be expressive of character: the character will be good if the purpose is good.[3]

This goodness differs from person to person, depending on their social level. Aristotle tells us that if a servant refrains from theft then he is good, but the same action does not matter in a gentleman, whose standards are different. Adam, when he gives all his savings to Orlando, shows his goodness and nobility of heart.

Appropriateness or Propriety signifies that a character should act or speak in accordance with the kind of character he is. Aristotle makes it clear by giving an example:

> There is a type of manly valour, but valour, in a woman, or unscrupulous cleverness, is inappropriate.[4]

Shakespeare does not deviate from this rule. The Duke, though in exile, is a nobleman in the full vigour of maturity. So he is ready to go hunting, and also keeps up the spirits of his followers. If he becomes dejected, so will they. So instead of repining he keeps smiling and this is much appreciated by his followers, as Amiens's remark about his "sweet" temper shows.

The third quality, Realism, has not been explained properly. Aristotle points out that this quality is different from goodness and propriety but he does not say much else except that the characters must be true to life. Shakespeare's characters are always so. Their actions and speech always suit the situation. M.C. Bradbrook says:

> Shakespeare's innovations in character-drawing may be compared to the introduction of perspective in painting: he gave the illusion of life. It was his characters which engaged the audiences of his own day.[5]

Consistency is the fourth quality demanded by Aristotle. This is the most important of all the four and means that the character must be true to his own personality. This is a rule based on human nature itself and Shakespeare never goes against nature. Now there are some cases of drastic changes of heart in the play which seem to be, on the surface, inconsistent. These cases of apparent inconsistency are Oliver's change of heart and that of Frederick's at the end of the play. Yet these are such that they do not really go against the rule of consistency, as shall be seen when their characters are analysed (*vide* Ch. 7, *infra*).

It is to be seen, thus, that two factors are to be kept in mind in delineating characters: the classical rules on one hand and the practical sketches provided by classical as well as English scholars. All these, as has been pointed out, were available to all the writers, yet Shakespeare gave more memorable characters than anyone else.

Many classifications of his characters have been given by modern scholars. The one given by L.S. Champion is suggestive and valuable. According to him Shakespeare depicts characters at the level appropriate to the story he is telling. The characters in the comedies suit the action of the play. If play is of a type that the stress is more on the action than on the characters (as in his early comedies like *The Comedy of Errors*) then the characters are sketchily depicted. It is different with the later comedies where the poet pays more attention to the characters and not so much to action. The characters are, accordingly, divided into three categories. The first is:

> The character who is delineated only on the level of "physical action", never inviting our response to him as an independent individual.[6]

This is not the case with the play under discussion, for *As You Like It* is not, like the early plays, a "situation comedy." Instead it is, as Champion calls it, a comedy of identity, in which human psychology is of more importance than action. The dramatist gradually develops the characters in terms of his or her reactions to situations in real life:

> In this situation the comic experience for the character is one of self-revelation.[7]

The characters of this play come under this category. Each character has to cope with the full bitterness of reality as it hits him or her. Orlando has to flee his home, depending on a servant for monetary help. When in the forest he meets the young shepherd-boy Ganymede he consents to play the game proposed by her. When he sees Oliver lying defenceless on the ground, about to he killed by a lioness, he forgets past injuries and springs to his defence. Thus, as the plot unfolds, each of the challenges hurled at him by fate reveals different facets of his personality. This happens to each of the characters, Orlando is merely a case in point.

The play is a mature play of Shakespeare and contains his best artistic efforts. It has been suggested by Bullough that basing his characters on Lodge's prose romance *Rosalynde*, Shakespeare divided his characters in *As You Like It* thus:

1. Figures of temporary evil: Oliver and Duke Frederick who represent "the evils of material world, intrinsic and malicious."
2. The courtiers of Duke Senior.
3. Rosalind, Celia and Orlando: "nobly born folk who are able to adjust themselves to the natural life of the country." The Duke Senior belongs here.
4. Silvius and Phoebe "who belong to the tradition of pastoral eclogues."
5. Corin, Audrey, William and Sir Oliver Martext "who reveal what country life, country people and country love are like at their most natural."[8]

Besides these he created four characters—Jaques, Touchstone, Audrey and William. All the characters in *As You Like It* are well-developed ones and have passed into the common literary knowledge of even people who are not scholars. The romantic hero and heroine apart, there are two other characters who can be called major ones—Duke senior, and Jaques the melancholy man. These characters shall be considered, in the same order as they appear in the list of *Dramatis Personae* in the text.

(B) DUKE SENIOR

We see the Senior Duke for the first time only in the second Act, but we have been told about him right in the first scene of the play. Charles the wrestler tells Oliver that the younger brother of the Duke has usurped his throne and driven him out of the kingdom. Some loyal lords have accompanied him in his exile and he is at present staying in the forest of Arden. Life in the forest is a merry life in beautiful pastoral surroundings. His daughter is left behind and it is from this daughter Rosalind, that we next hear of him. She is out of spirits because she is missing her father. In other words, Shakespeare tells us that the Duke was a loving father and had a true paternal relationship with his daughter, which, quite often, is absent in aristocratic families.

Later we see that she is attracted towards Orlando and when she learns that her own father and Orlando's father were intimate friends this knowledge enhances her feelings toward him. Again, indirectly, we are told that the Duke had a loving disposition. He was capable of inspiring devotion and loyalty in others.

She is banished by Frederick in the very next scene and Celia decides that they shall set forth on a journey to join Duke senior in the forest of Arden. In other words they feel sure that he will accord a kind welcome to his daughter and niece which is more than what Frederick has done.

Thus when we meet the Duke in the wood we already know that he is a loving father, a loving friend and a loved leader also, as many of his lords have followed him to the forest and left their property and family behind them.

Shakespeare has given him one of his best passages. The Duke knows through experience that forest life is not all merriment and comfort. It is true that mother nature is benevolent but at times she can be harsh also. She does not treat with indulgence aristocrats brought up in luxury. During winter it is bitterly cold:

> the icy fang
> And churlish chiding of the winter's wind,

> Which, when it is bites and blows upon my body
> Even till I shrink with cold.

The Duke is not daunted by this stern aspect of nature. Indeed, he prefers it to life at court, for there dangers are hidden by hypocrisy, but here all dangers are in the open. He welcomes a harsh life for another reason—privation and danger give moral upliftment to one's character:

> And this our life, exempt from public haunt
> Finds tongues in trees, books in running brooks,
> Sermons in stones and good in everything.[10]

We admire the sweet temper of the Duke, his wisdom and his ability to adjust himself to suit his surroundings. Hazlitt has singled out these particular lines to express his admiration of the tone and style of the Duke. He exclaims:

> Never was there such beautiful moralizing, equally free from pedantry or petulance.[11]

In this speech Shakespeare shows the Duke contrasting court life with forest life and in the next dwells on a significant theme. This speech, indeed, enhances our respect for him. He begins by saying that they will go hunting. Now, hunting is a royal sport and the Duke seems to be quite light-hearted and looking forward to an enjoyable day with his loyal lords. The vicissitudes of life, however, have already engendered pity for the poor unfortunate persons in his soul. He thinks of the hunted and wounded deer who are the rightful dwellers of the forest. He has usurped their kingdom just as his brother has usurped his:

> And yet it irks me the poor dappled fools,
> Being native burghers of this desert city
> Should in their own confines with forked heads,
> Have their round haunches gored.[12]

Shakespeare shows how adversity has expanded his character to include hunted animals in his sympathy for the unfortunate. We do not know what kind of a person he had been before he came to the forest but it goes without saying that forest life has broadened his outlook. This is also seen when Orlando interrupts his feast in Act II, sc. vii. Instead of haughtily reprimanding Orlando, as would be but natural for him, he first wants to know the circumstances and when Orlando says he is hungry, at once, with royal dignity and real nobility he invites Orlando to sit and eat. When Orlando tells him about Adam he at once tells him to bring Adam and assures him that they will not eat till he comes. There was no need for him to make this promise. It is his innate gentleness that prompts him to do so.

After this the dramatist concentrates on the other characters. We see him next only in the last scene. Here, like the beloved father-figure that he is, he presides over the entire scene. When Hymen hands him his daughter he readily acknowledges her. He had already remarked earlier in the scene that Rosalind-Ganymede resembled his daughter and now that he sees her he makes no difference in his welcome to her and his niece. There is not a mean bone in his body—he welcomes the daughter of his treacherous brother with open arms.

When Jaques de Boys brings the welcome news of the restoration of his kingdom he receives the news with becoming dignity and orders for the commencement of music and dancing so that the spirit of festivities may be redoubled.

In quite a few of his plays Shakespeare gives us a world in which the older generation does not exist (*Merchant of Venice*, *Twelfth Night*). Here he presents the older generation as a figure of dignity and benevolence. The Duke's situation has been compared with that of king Lear and Prospero. There are definite similarities. Lear is a tragic figure, but he too was shown as gaining sympathy for "poor wretched creatures" through his own misery just as the Duke sympathizes with the hunted deer. Lear had also been arrogant and foolish and had to be purged of these traits by being plunged into misery. Shakespeare has been kinder to the Duke. He too has to undergo betrayal and misery, but these are not as severe as Lear's. Moreover, as the play is a comedy it would have been most improper to have evoked the pity and terror that Lear does evoke. The comparison with Prospero also can only be a superficial one. Like Prospero, the Duke too has been betrayed by a younger brother and has withdrawn into a world of beauty, but here the resemblance ends. The Duke has his Lords about him, not alone with a baby daughter like Prospero. Moreover, Prospero rules the natural and the supernatural world with his magical powers whereas the Duke rules his followers with and through love. He is a man among men and Prospero is a mage among spirits.

It is also said that the Duke and Jaques complement each other:

> Jaques and the Duke are clearly intended as doublets or complementaries: *Il penseroso* and *L'allegro*, the weeping and the laughing philosopher.[13]

This interpretation of the Duke elevates him to a symbolic or allegorical figure. Shakespeare has created many father-figures and the Duke is the most genial and attractive of them.

(C) JAQUES

Jaques is the first of the four characters whom Shakespeare has added to Lodge's romance, the other three being Touchstone, Audrey and William. He is the well-known "melancholy man" of Elizabethan times and shows how Shakespeare can adopt the conventions of his own time to add to the dramatic value of his plays. This character has been studied in detail and many are the interpretations available on him.

We see him first in Act II, sc. v but his entrance has been prepared for in Act II, sc. i in which the first Lord described how he moralized over a wounded deer. His first appearance is a very quiet one. The scene starts with the focus on Amiens who sings the famous song "under the greenwood tree." After he has sung the first stanza Jaques requests him to sing the second and Amiens complies. Then Jaques gives the parody of the song, "If it do come to pass", etc. It has been said that here he is mocking the lords who have accompanied the Duke, leaving their courtly life of ease and luxury. His sentences are all full of hints and innuendoes. For example, when he says he will "rail against all the first born of Egypt" he is referring to the Duke who according to the laws of primogeniture had inherited his kingdom but who, like the first born of Egypt (this is a Biblical reference) has been deprived of his inheritance.

In the next scene he is in a merry mood, for he has met Touchstone. He describes the meeting in detail to Duke Senior, saying again and again that he himself would like to be a fool:

> O that I were a fool
> I am ambitious for a motley coat.[14]

He gives the reasons for this desire. A fool is the only person in the court who has freedom of speech:

> I must have liberty
> Withal, as large a charter as the wind,
> To blow on whom I please, for so fools have
> And they that are most galled with my folly,
> They most must love.[15]

This is a most important speech and brings out the satirical bent of Jaques's mind.

This speech is followed by another famous one in which he anatomizes human nature with all its vanities and hypocrisies. These three are some of the keenest satirical passages in Shakespeare. Everything is said lightly yet they expose the weakness of man and society most effectively. It is particularly with reference to these lines that Jaques has been thought to represent Ben Jonson. While not fully agreeing with this view John Dover Wilson partially supports it:

> Jaques may certainly be taken in some ways standing for the Johnsonian point of view—the critical standpoint.[16]

After this, when Orlando has gone for Adam Jaques holds the stage with one of the most celebrated passages in Shakespeare, "All the world's a stage." This passage with its image (or metaphor) taken from the theatrical world has been repeatedly analysed and commented upon. He compares man with an actor who acts out the different phases of his life on the stage, i.e., the world. Presenting graphic pictures of each stage of life, it is a masterpiece of description. It is a set-piece, put in to fill the gap in the action while the audience is waiting for Orlando to return. Very often such gaps are filled in by songs. It is only Shakespeare who would dare to put such a significant passage merely to fill up a gap and make a resounding success out of it.

We see Jaques next in Act III, sc. iii, conversing with Orlando. It is a witty dialogue in which he is laughing at Orlando's lovelorn state but Orlando has no mind for his company. Jaques represents the detached man's amused reaction at the antics of a romantic lover.

In Act III, sc. iii, also, following Touchstone and Audrey, he keeps up this role of a detached observer. But he shows himself to be tolerant and co-operative when the priest will not marry them for the lack of someone to give away the bride. He offers himself for this work and later offers Touchstone good advice about his marriage. However, much of a satirical observer Shakespeare might have made him, he has not made Jaques inhumanly detached.

In Act IV, sc. i, while trying to make a friend of Rosalind-Ganymede, he gives the best account of his melancholy nature that can be found:

> It is a melancholy of mine own, compounded of many simples, extracted from many objects and indeed the sundry contemplation of my travels.[17]

This makes it clear that he is no self-deceived fool. He is as much an observer of his own nature as that of others.

He shows himself to be a good Master of ceremonies in a quite impromptu manner in the hunting-scene (Act IV, sc. ii). He proposes that the man who killed the deer should be crowned and borne in triumph to the Duke. This is done in a most entertaining manner, affording opportunity for the element of spectacle (*vide* Ch. 4, *supra*).

After this he appears in the last scene. Here, again, with Touchstone, he serves to fill up a gap in the action when Rosalind-Ganymede and Celia go offstage to put away their disguises. It is a witty dialogue in which Touchstone explains different kinds of lies with Jaques to help him on with questions and comments.

When he speaks next it is to renounce courtly life in favour of a contemplative one, with Duke Frederick:

> To him will I: out of these convertites
> There is much matter to be heard and learned.[18]

Bidding farewell to everyone, he leaves the stage.

From one point of view his is a simple, and from another a complex character. First of all he is the melancholy man who is a typical figure of the time, explained by Overbury, Newton, Hall and others. Overbury gives a long description:

> ...a strayer from the drove.... He thinkes businesse, but never doeth any: he is all contemplation, no action. He hewes and fashions his thoughts, as if he meant them to some purpose but they prove unprofitable.[19]

Jaques' character is true to this description. Yet he is not merely a melancholy man, but an example of how Shakespeare takes up a fixed type and gives it a distinct individuality of its own. Jaques's melancholy does not harm any one:

> ...his melancholy is a source of pleasure and amusement to others. The Duke treats him virtually as a court enteretainer.[20]

In like manner, Dowden has pointed out that there is no melancholy in the real sense in him. It is but the result of a personal idiosyncracy. This view is supported by Jaques himself in the speech to Rosalind when he explains the nature of his melancholy in a long sentence.[21] It is very much the same kind of unaccountable melancholy as that of Antonio on *The Merchant of Venice.*

There is also another aspect of his melancholy that Hazlitt had perceived and pointed out:

> Jaques is the only purely contemplative character in Shakespeare. He thinks, and does nothing.[22]

In fact it is the word "contemplative" that is more suited to him than melancholy, as is shown when he opts for a hermit's life. The desire to leave the world and become a hermit was perhaps hidden within him from before and as soon as he hears of Frederick's conversion he too turns to a life of contemplation rather than return to the court.

As has been observed above (*vide* the character of the Duke, *supra*) there is a clear contrast between Duke Senior and Jaques, the former being the laughing philosopher and the latter a weeping one. It is significant that this critic makes use of the same terms (*L'allegro* and *Il penseroso*) as Milton uses in his two famous poems with these names. He, giving a sketch of the latter, expressly pointed out that such a man, in his old age, lives the life of a hermit.

(D) ORLANDO

Orlando is the typical romantic hero. In the full flower of youth and beauty, he captivates Rosalind and finally leads her to the altar, thus fulfilling the aims of a romantic comedy. He is, indeed the most captivating of Shakespeare's romantic heroes. He may not he as witty as Lord Berowne or Benedick, but he is far more gentle and generous, as his devotion to old Adam proves.

It is to him that Shakespeare gives the honour of opening the play. He speaks in prose and it is an expository passage acquainting the reader with his background. He is extremely resentful to his brother for not giving him his due and he wonders how to break free. There is a scuffle between the brothers in which Orlando takes Oliver by the throat. Besides emphasizing the bad relationship between the two brothers, this incident also highlights Orlando's great physical strength which prepares the reader for his victory in the wrestling-match.

When, in the next scene he meets Rosalind and Celia it is notable that he behaves just as a young nobleman should. He had complained that he had not received the upbringing proper to a noble young man, yet there is no gaucherie in him.

After he wins the match Frederick, instead of rewarding him rebuffs him on learning his father's name. He might have become dejected at all this, but everything becomes immaterial because he falls in love with Rosalind. While she and Celia talk to him he stands tongue-tied and when they leave he is surprised at himself:

> Can I not say, "I thank you?" My better parts
> Are all thrown down and that which here stands up
> Is but a quintain, a mere lifeless block.[23]

By the time that Le Beau comes he has mastered himself enough to attend to him and thank him for the information and advice he receives. He asks Le Beau about the two princesses and realizes that it is with Rosalind, the daughter of Duke Senior, that he has fallen in love in such a precipitate manner.

This kind of love at first sight is not at all rare in literature. In this play itself there are two pairs who fall in love at first sight for later Oliver and Celia also fall in love with each other in the same manner. Phoebe also falls in love with Ganymede, but her love cannot be considered seriously, though it is she who quotes Marlowe's famous lines.

Orlando's sudden love for Rosalind is to be found in Lodge's romance as well. Rosader, his counterpart, sees Rosalynde at a tournament and falls in love:

> ...forgetting himself, he stoode and fed his lookes on the favour of Rosalynde's face.[24]

It is an experience that changes the entire life of a young man or girl. He leaves the palace and starts for home with no thoughts but of his blinding, all-consuming love in his mind.

Before reaching home he is intercepted by the old servant Adam and, coming to know that his brother is out for his blood he leaves home, taking Adam with him.

When we see them next, in Act II, sc. vi, they are near the forest. No other scene brings the true nobility of his character to the focus as this scene does. Adam, tired, cannot walk any further and asks Orlando to abandon him. Orlando, however, with true affection, takes him to the shelter of the woods and sets out in quest of food. He had complained that Oliver had denied him the upbringing of a gentleman, but here he shows the true inborn nobility that needs no education. He could not have done more for Adam if he had been his father.

Then in the banquet scene he appears with a drawn sword in hand. But the innate gentleness of his nature asserts itself as soon as the Duke speaks kindly to him. Then, in an eloquent speech he asks Duke Senior to give him some food for his old servant. He does not eat, though he is hungry but goes away to fetch Adam. Once more his love for and loyalty towards the servant is manifest. He is not ashamed to tell the assembled company that Adam is just a servant, for he has no false pride.

At length fortune smiles at him for he joins the Duke's retinue. He is now free of care and in good company. Time is ripe for love to blossom.

Like a Petrarchan lover, he writes verses to Rosalind and hangs them upon the branches of trees. In Lodge also, after receiving a jewel from Rosalynde, Rosader writes verses to her. Jaques mocks at him for being so lovelorn and Orlando gives tit for tat:

Jaques: The worst fault you have is to be in love

Or: 'Tis a fault I will not change for your best virtue... I am weary of you.

J: By my troth, I was seeking for a fool when I found you.

O: He is drowned in the brook—look but in and you shall see him.[25]

He meets Rosalind immediately after this, but of course he does not know her identity. He is won over by this charming young man. This again is proof of his good nature, for instead of rebuffing a forward youth he indulges him.

Then his lessons in love begin. Gently, as in a game, Rosalind proceeds to make his love less other-worldly and more realistic. Marriage is a great responsibility and Orlando has to be prepared for it:

Ros.: Well, in her person, I say I will not have you.

Or.: Then, in mine own person, I die.[26]

Then Rosalind, with gentle mockery, makes him realise that such violent protests are unrealistic:

> Men have died from time to time, and worms have eaten them, but not for love.[27]

This is the only such scene we see, but the love-game has been going on for quite some time. He then promises to come and meet her in two hours' time.

His singularly noble action in saving Oliver's life is reported by Oliver himself. This act of brotherly love brings about a total change of heart in Oliver Orlando thus saves more than Oliver's life. He changes Oliver from a villain into a normal man.

When he hears of Oliver's impending marriage he is naturally downcast in spirits and confides his "heart-heaviness" to Rosalind-Ganymede. He replies to her light-heated repartee in a short and significant sentence: "I can live no loner by thinking."[28] He is no longer the lovelorn impractical youth he was. His love has matured and realizing this Rosalind prepares him for the next day.

His promise to marry Rosalind is repeated the next day in front of everyone and when the time comes he accepts her without hesitation: "If there be truth in sight, you are my Rosalind."[29] Thus is the true aim of romantic comedy achieved.

Shakespeare, thus, develops his character from that of a resentful young man into a thoughtful, responsible member of society, from an infatuated lover into a deeply sincere one:

> In Rosalind and Orlando of *As You Like It* the dramatist again depicts a growth in the comprehension of love which leads them to a fuller realization of their true personalities.[30]

He enters Arden a footsore, hungry young man burdened with the responsibility of an old man, and he leaves it a prosperous and happily married man. The forest of Arden, by bringing his love to maturity, changes his personality:

> Obviously then, through the catalyst of love, Orlando's personality is purged and his highest qualities realized.[31]

(E) ROSALIND

No other Shakespearean heroine is quite so popular as Rosalind. This too is one of those characters developed by being subjected to many kinds of experiences. These are not harrowing ones for Rosalind's character does not have such flaws as have to be purged through sorrow and misery. It is she, on the other hand, who prepares Orlando for a mature concept of love and teaches Phoebe a lesson.

The cataclysmic experience of falling in love, followed by her cruel banishment, leaves her bewildered at first but soon enough, helped by Celia, she picks up her spirits and develops into one of the most charming heroines of Shakespeare. She decides to disguise herself as the shepherd-boy Ganymede, very like Portia when the latter talks of putting on the disguise of a lawyer.

By the time they arrive near the forest all three of them are tired. She takes her part as a young man quite seriously and though admitting to being tired she does not succumb to weariness but tries to encourage Celia. She it is who takes the decision to buy the cottage, etc. and keep Corin on to look after the flock of sheep. Shakespeare gives her presence of mind and the ability to take a quick decision.

The softer side of her nature—that of a young girl in love, is revealed in Act III, sc. ii. She importunes Celia to her about her meeting with Orlando:

> Alas the day, what shall I do with my doublet and hose? What did he when thou saw'st him? What said he? How looked he? Wherein went he? What makes he here? Did he ask for me? Where remains he? How parted he with thee? When shalt thou see him again? Answer me in one word.[32]

It does not take her long to recover herself and when she accosts Orlando it is with full self-confidence. Then she proposes to cure him of this disease of love by playing a game.

Before the scene of this love-game, however, there comes another scene, revealing another facet of her character—a sensible, no-nonsense aspect. She sees Phoebe spurning Silvius and gives her the famous advice:

> But mistress, know yourself—down on your knees,
> And thank heaven, fasting, for a good man's love.[33]

Unfortunately for Phoebe, she falls in love with Rosalind-Ganymede, which Rosalind herself perceives at once. The scene clarifies her own attitude—that instead of being vain and scornful one should be grateful if one is loved by a good man.

In the charming scene of love-game we see an entirely feminine aspect of her character. She curbs Orlando's violent protestations and brings him closer to a more practical view of love.

The stern moral preceptress comes to the front once more when Silvius brings her Phoebe's letter and she tries to open Silvius' eyes to her deceitfulness:

> Wilt thou love such a woman?
> What, to make thee an instrument and
> play false strains upon thee![34]

Again a wholly feminine side comes to the front when she learns about Orlando's exploits with the lioness, but by the time that she meets him she has recovered herself enough to joke with him. Then, she, with her womanly intuition, realizes that Orlando's time of apprenticeship in love has come to an end. The time for sport is over and she now changes her tactics. The plan she has formed is helped along by that pair of disgruntled lover, Silvius and Phoebe, and she fixes the next morning for finding a solution to all their problems.

Again, this shows the quickness with which she can alter her plans to suit the circumstances. At first when she makes her promise to Orlando, she has no thoughts of the shepherd couple but she quickly includes them in her plans when they arrive.

The last scene shows her triumph. One admires, not merely the way in which she makes the act of revealing her identity result in her own union with Orlando, but also that of Silvius and Phoebe. It is a resourceful, economical move that achieves a two-fold result. When she enters with Hymen in the full glory of her womanhood she wastes no time. Explaining the position briefly and succinctly, she surrenders herself first to her father, then to Orlando.

> Ras.: (*to the Duke*) To you I give myself for I am yours.
> (*to Orlando*) To you I give myself for I am yours.[35]

It is noticeable that she uses the same words to surrender herself to the Duke as to Orlando. This is but right and proper, for the rights of a father over his daughter are supreme, but so is that of husband after the marriage. So she addresses the one who had authority over her in the past, and then the one who shall have it in future.

Except for a short three-line speech to Phoebe she does not speak again in the rest of the play. But in an extraordinary manner, Shakespeare gives her the Epilogue. It should be remembered that she is the only female character in the whole of Shakespeare to deliver an Epilogue. This Epilogue is a light-hearted and witty prose passage. First of all she says that it is unusual for a lady to deliver the Epilogue and then playfully remarks that it is no more incongruous than to see a lord delivering the Prologue. After a few more such sentences she exhorts the audience to express their approval of the play:

> I charge you, O women, for the love you bear to men, to like as much of this play as please you: and I charge you, O men, for the love you bear to women—as I perceive by your simpering, none of you hates them—that between you and the women the play may please.[36]

Even in this Epilogue, Rosalind's sparkling wit and high spirits are amply in evidence. It is typical of her and typical of a romantic comedy, that the theme of love should be repeated even in the Epilogue, as also, incidentally, the name of the play, in an indirect manner.

Rosalind, throughout, is presented as a witty, high-spirited and resourceful woman who, beneath all her wit, has a soft, feminine heart that is capable of giving warm and generous love to all. Withal, she is a practical, down-to-earth person who is ready to face all the challenges of reality. H.B. Charlton, analysing the heroines of Shakespeare, comes to the conclusion that it was only in women that Shakespeare found a balanced and harmonious personality. Warmth of heart and intuitive insight are wedded in their character. Hand-in-hand with this goes a fine mother-wit or common sense:

> Instinct and intuition were guided by a mind in which a sublimated common sense had established itself as the habitual director of action and behaviour.[37]

The presence of this intuitive insight and sublimated common sense is to be seen again and again in Rosalind—in the way in which she tackles the problems she faces particularly that of Phoebe.

In so far as the cheerfulness and gaiety of her temperament are concerned, this has been pointed out from a very early time. But a thoughtful look had been cast in this direction in the nineteenth century when it had been remarked:

> The characters of the banished Duke, of Orlando, of Rosalind, are described as three gradation of cheerfulness in adversity.[38]

This gives a symbolic elevation to the character of Rosalind as well as those of the other two. At the other extreme is the opinion of John Dover Wilson who equates Rosalind with the modern woman:

> In Rosalind we have a prophetic adumbration of the gallant girls of our own time, full of the spirit of adventure...yet passionately devoted to the service of mankind.[39]

Rosalind, as a matter of fact, has charmed both the audience and the reader ever since she came into being, leaping into life with each word. It has always been, and is even now, the ambition of all actresses to play this role.

Such, therefore, are the major characters of the play—each a fully individualized, living convincing creature. We shall see how he pays no less attention to the minor characters. In each case he follows his original source, contemporary stage conventions as well as classical rules and turns them to his own advantage as no other contemporary writer could.

REFERENCES

1. Quoted by Fluchère, *op. cit.*, p. 131.
2. *Ibid.*, p. 136.
3. Butcher, S.H., *Aristotle's Theory of Poetry and Fine Art with a Critical Text Translation of The Poetics*, New Delhi, Kalyani Publishers, 1981, Ch. 15, p. 53.

4. *Ibid.*
5. Bradbrook, M.C., *Growth and Structure of Elizabethan Comedy*, London, Chatto and Windus, 1955, p. 80.
6. Champion, L.S., *op. cit.*, p. 8.
7. *Ibid.*
8. Bullough, Geoffrey, *Narrative and Dramatic Sources of Shakespeare*, Vol. II, London, Routledge and Kegan Paul, 1969, pp. 153-56.
9. Act II, sc. i, ll. 6-9, p. 22.
10. Act II, sc. i, ll. 15-17, p. 22.
11. Hazlitt, W., *On As You Like It*, in Russell, J.B., *op. cit.*, p. 33.
12. Act II, sc. i, ll. 21-25, p. 22.
13. Hawkins, Sherman, *op. cit.*, p. 66.
14. Act II, sc. vii, ll. 42-43, p. 35.
15. Act II, sc. vii, ll. 47-51, p. 35.
16. Wilson, J.D., *op. cit.*, p. 153.
17. Act IV, sc. i, ll. 15-18, p. 64.
18. Act V, sc. iv, ll. 181-82, p. 90.
19. Brown, John Russell, *op. cit.*, p. 208.
20. Gardner, Helen, *op. cit.*, p. 164.
21. Act IV, sc. i, ll. 10-17, p. 64.
22. Brown, *op. cit.*, p. 33.
23. Act I, sc. ii, ll. 237-39, p. 15.
24. Bullough, G., *op. cit.*, p. 171.
25. Act III, sc. ii, ll. 279-85, p. 49.
26. Act IV, sc. i, ll. 88-89, p. 66.
27. Act IV, sc. i, ll. 101-03, p. 66.
28. Act V, sc. ii, l. 58, p. 80.
29. Act V, sc. ii, l. 116, p. 88.
30. Champion, L.S., *op. cit.*, p. 65.
31. *Ibid.*, p. 66.
32. Act III, sc. ii, ll. 217-22, p. 47.
33. Act III, sc. v, ll. 57-58, p. 61.
34. Act IV, sc. iii, ll. 66-69, p. 73.
35. Act IV, sc. iv, ll. 113-14, p. 88.
36. Epilogue, ll. 11-16, p. 92.
37. Charlton, H.B., *op. cit.*, p. 286.
38. Brown, *op. cit.*, p. 36.
39. Wilson, *op. cit.*, p. 162.

7

The Minor Characters

As has been observed in the last chapter, our poet did not neglect his minor characters. Most of the other playwrights of his time created one or two memorable characters in their plays and the others were like shadowy outlines, not well drawn, living portraits. This is the case, most notably, with Marlowe. Shakespeare's characters, even the minor ones, however, are convincing rounded-out figures. This may not be true of his early plays, but by the time he was writing the golden comedies those works of apprenticeship were left behind. The minor characters of the play under discussion provide the relevant social background and help to take the action forward. There are many of them (no less than sixteen), and Shakespeare has endowed each of them with his or her own distinct individuality. They shall now be considered in the same order as given in the *Dramatis Personae* of the text.

(i) Duke Frederick

Duke Frederick is one of the play's important minor characters. His role in the beginning is very much like that of Antonio in *The Tempest* who usurps Prospero's kingdom and sets him and Miranda adrift in the ocean. Shakespeare, however, has treated Frederick much more kindly. Though Frederick is a villain throughout the play he undergoes a total change of heart at the end which is reported by Jaques de Boys, and not shown on the stage. Antonio, on the other hand, remains an unmitigated villain.

He shows himself in a very unfavourable light right from the beginning, when he turns against Orlando merely because

Orlando's father was the dearest friend of Rosalind's father. Instead of praising and rewarding Orlando he turns away from him in a manner which can only be called churlish. Then in the next scene he banishes his niece Rosalind without any fault, or, indeed, any cause at all: "Thou art thy father's daughter, there's enough",[1] says he in answer to Rosalind's pleadings.

When we see him next he is busy instituting a search for the girls and for Orlando. He orders Oliver to be brought to him if Orlando cannot be found and this is done in Act III, sc. i. Here he shows himself to be a typical tyrant. He confiscates the land and property of Oliver and tells him not to come back to him unless he can catch Orlando within a year. After this we do not see him any more in the play.

Even though he does not appear on the stage again, he helps to bring a bout a happy ending right in the last scene by being converted to a religious life. Jaques de Boys, the second son of Sir Rowland de Boys, comes in the last scene to give Duke Senior the news of his conversion. Frederick was coming to the forest of Arden with an army, intending to kill Duke Senior, but God had pity on him and saved him from fratricide:

> Where, meeting with an old religious man,
> After some question with him, was converted
> Both from his enterprise and from the world.[2]

Thus, at the very last moment he restores to the Duke his rightful inheritance whose life in the forest comes to an end and so does the play.

This sudden conversion is very convenient from the point of view of dramatic strategy, but the question arises, is this realistic or consistent with the psychological portrayal of the character? It is true that Shakespeare very often does not pay much heed to classical rules. The play is more important to him than any rules can be. In this instance, however, Frederick's conversion can be fully justified. As far as realism goes, Shakespeare has already portrayed Frederick as a character who is subject to sudden and unpredictable changes of moods. Le Beau, advising Orlando to leave the court, hints as much:

> The Duke is humorous—what he is, indeed,
> More suits you to conceive than I to speak of.[3]

A few lines later he again says that Frederick has taken a dislike to Rosalind and that it might lead to serious consequences:

> of late this duke
> Hath ta'en displeasure 'gainst his gentle niece.
> ....
> And on my life, his malice 'gainst the lady.
> Will suddenly break forth.[4]

One gets the impression that the Duke is not only of a tyrannical disposition but one who is quite likely to change his mood suddenly. It would not be surprising therefore that he should equally suddenly decide to leave courtly life and, renouncing everything, adopt the life of a hermit.

Moreover, such sudden conversions are not at all impossible where religion is concerned. Thus, Sylvan Barnet, discussing the "strange" or "improbable" events in the play, analyses Oliver's and Frederick's conversions:

> Like Oliver's conversion, Frederick's is apparently triggered by a sudden experience and has "an element of marvellous."[5]

The lives of the saints provide ample examples of such conversion. The most famous of these is the case of St. Paul God's grace can rain down upon anyone and make a saint out of a villain, quite without any reason or any prior indications. This conversion thus is explicable and acceptable from the religious as well as psychological point of view. (In this connection *vide* the discussion on Oliver, *infra.*)

(ii) Amiens

Amiens is one of the lords who have accompanied Duke Senior to the forest. He is a singer and provides the much-needed element of music in the play. He speaks very little and indeed it is the songs he sings that mark him out. On his first appearance he is with the Duke and praises his fortitude:

Happy is your grace
That can translate the stubbornness of fortune
Into so quiet and so sweet a style.[6]

This is no sycophancy but heart-felt admiration. He makes the audience appreciate the Duke's calm acceptance of adversity by appreciating it himself.

After this we see him in Act II, sc. v, in which he opens the scene with the famous song:

Under the greenwood tree,
Who loves to lie with me,
And turn his merry note
Unto the sweet bird's throat...
Come hither, come hither, come hither.[7]

He sings only one stanza and Jaques has to persuade him to sing the second. He allows himself to be cajoled into completing the song. Jaques then sings a parody of it. Though it is not clear whether Amiens resents this mockery or not, yet it seems that perhaps he does not, for he good-naturedly offers to sing it.

After this in the banquet-scene (Act II, sc. vii) he sings another melodious song:

Blow, blow, thou winter wind,
Thou art not so unkind
As man's ingratitude.[8]

He sings the song to the Duke's request ("good cousin, sing") but otherwise he does not speak in the scene. It is noticeable, however, that he has chosen a song that suits the Duke's mood to perfection.

In the hunting-scene he speaks just two words, in answer to Jaques' question whether he has a song for this occasion or not and then sings the triumph-song in which the others join.

After this, though he is present on the stage he does not speak or sing. His main function in the play is to provide entertainment through vocal music. It is this that lends individuality to his character. Music is one of the important elements of drama (*vide* Ch. 10, *infra*) and as he sings two of the important songs in the play he stands out from the rest of the Duke's retinue. Both of the first two songs, in addition to their entertainment value, are of great importance as they successfully create the pastoral atmosphere so necessary to the play.

(iii) Le Beau

Le Beau is the only one of Duke Frederick's courtiers who has a proper speaking part. It is true that two other lords also speak in a later scene, but their role is negligible as they speak only a few lines. We see Le Beau in only one scene (Act I, sc. ii), but he leaves the impression of being a wise and kindly lord. In other words, he is an individualized character.

He comes to tell the two princesses of the Duke's summons to them to witness the wrestling-match that they have missed. They interrupt him at every sentence but he does not lose his temper and tells how Charles has already overthrown three young men and also broken their ribs. Then he informs them that the rest of the match will take place just where they are standing. Though they and Touchstone speak very lightly, almost mockingly to him, yet he is such a polished courtier that he does not reprove them.

It is after the wrestling-match is over that Le Beau reveals his individuality. He has great sympathy for the personable unfortunate young man, Orlando. Taking pity on him, he comes and gives Orlando good advice. He knows Duke Frederick and fears the worst. So he comes and warns Orlando against Frederick, telling him to flee the court at once. He is no sycophant, but nor does he criticize the Duke openly to Orlando, which is an indication of his loyalty to his master—be he good or bad. He gives indications of his disapproval of the Duke's ugly mood and churlish behaviour, but indirectly:

> The duke is humorous—what he is, indeed
> More suits you to conceive than I to speak of.[9]

Again in answer to Orlando's question about which of the two princesses is the daughter of Frederick he says "Neither his daughter, if we judge by manners."[10] Such oblique words signify his disapproval of Frederick, but, like a good courtier, he does not criticize his master in front of an outsider.

In this one and only appearance Le Beau serves several important purposes. First of all he warns Orlando against Frederick. Secondly he identifies Rosalind as Duke Senior's daughter and thirdly he tells Orlando of Frederick's anger against his own niece, thus preparing the audience for the summary way in which he is to banish her in the very next scene. He shows himself to be a kind soul who, though loyal to his master, is by no means blind to his faults.

(iv) Charles

Charles is the wrestler in the court of Frederick. He has two appearances in the play and comes first in the very first scene, to tell Oliver about the wrestling-match to be held at the Duke's court. He has come to know that Orlando is going to enter the competition and he wants to know Oliver's attitude. He gives Oliver all the news of the court and Oliver then tells him that there is no need for him to worry about his feelings regarding Orlando—he may do as he likes.

After this dialogue with Oliver he hardly speaks again in the play. He only says two sentences in the next scene before the match and then he is defeated and carried out unconscious.

He is a very minor character but he serves several important purposes. It is he who informs Oliver about the banishment of the elder Duke and his withdrawal into the forest of Arden; preparing the audience for the pastoral environment to be introduced later:

> They say he is already in the forest of Arden, and a many merry men with him; ...and fleet the time carelessly as they did in the golden world.[11]

Next, he also provides the element of spectacle (*opsis*) in the play through the wrestling-match, which is one of the classical requirements for a play. There are three such occasions and Charles provides the first of them.

(v) Oliver

Oliver, the elder brother of Orlando, is the most important of the minor characters. Not only does he influence the hero at the two most crucial points in the play but thereby influence the action as well. He and Duke Frederick make up the team of villains in the play and have many features in common between the two of them.

Just as there is no true cause for the ugly behaviour of Frederick, so is there no real cause for the hatred that Oliver bears towards Orlando. In both of the cases Shakespeare has tried to justify this hatred by telling us that both are envious. So, just as Frederick has dispossessed his elder brother and driven him from home, Oliver also tries to kill Orlando which forces him to leave his home. When he is in turn driven out by Frederick he reaches the forest of Arden "A wretched ragged man, O'ergrown with hair" and here the first of his conversions occurs.

Orlando, out of sheer goodness of heart and inborn nobility saves his life and this brings about a total change of heart in Oliver. He himself is aware of the fact that this has made a different man of him:

> 'Twas I; but 'tis not I: I do not shame
> To tell you what I was, since my conversion
> So sweetly tastes, being the thing I am.[12]

Thus does Orlando's nobility changes a villain into a penitent. Yet this is not the end, for another important change occurs in his personality—he falls in love with Celia. This is the third case of love at first sight in the play. Rosalind and Orlando fall in love with each other at first sight, then Phoebe falls in love with Rosalind-Ganymede and now Oliver and Celia fall in love with each other. They make up the fourth pair of lovers, Silvius and Phoebe being another—the second in order of appearance. These cases of love at first sight have been extensively commented upon—particularly that of Rosalind and Orlando. Dr. Johnson had suggested that Shakespeare is nearing the end of the play and therefore quickly winds up the plot. It has also been suggested that these two important changes in Oliver have been brought about in such a hasty manner because Shakespeare does not want us to pay any attention to them. John Wain says:

> The double conversion of the two villainous characters, Duke Frederick and Orlando's brother Oliver, is sketched

> in with a perfunctoriness that saves the play, perhaps, from ridicule; if Shakespeare had not shown us so plainly that he did not care whether we believed in the story or not, if he had made it even a shade more credible, we might have tried to believe in it.[13]

The upshot of both of these changes in him is that not only is harmony restored in the family, but also Oliver is prepared for a sylvan life. He decides not to go back to his palace but live in the forest with Celia, leading the simple life of shepherds. He bequeaths his land and property to Orlando so that Orlando can go back and lead the life of a married nobleman. His change of heart brings about as great a change in his own life as Frederick's does in his.

(vi) Jaques de Boys

This young man is the second son of Sir Rowland de Boys, Oliver being the first and Orlando the third. We see him only in the last scene. He is the brother whom Oliver has kept at school though he denies any kind of education to Orlando. This is mentioned by Orlando in the first scene. Then in the last scene, after the masque is over and the lovers have been paired off, he makes his entry to announce the fact that Duke Frederick has renounced the world, and adopted a hermit's life:

> met with an old religious man,
> After some question with him was converted
> Both from his enterprise and from the world:
> His crown bequeathing to his banished brother
> And all their lands restored to them again
> That were with him exited.[14]

Thus, in a few succinct words he explains the position and thereby brings about a total change in the lives of the characters. He is a highly useful and functional character who crucially changes the action and brings about the happy ending of the play. The four marriages by themselves bring about a happy ending, but for the lovers only. Jaques de Boys brings happiness to the older men also. Now the Duke with all his followers will be able to go back to his kingdom and the future of the hero and the heroine is established firmly.

Jaques de Boys, as a matter of fact, is a *deus ex machina* who serves to bring about the desired happy ending of a play by smoothing out all the difficulties. It is true that he himself does not do anything but acts as just a messenger, but his message itself has the same action as a *deus ex machina* has in a play.

(vii) Adam

Adam the old servant is a symbol of self-sacrifice and loyalty. He had been in the service of Sir Rowland and is now in the household of his son. He criticizes Oliver with the privilege that old servants have:

> God be with my old master! he would not have spoke such a word.[15]

He keeps watch over Orlando and as soon as he returns from the wrestling-match meets him at the orchard adjacent to the house to warn him of Oliver's murderous intentions. Knowing that Orlando does not have any money he gives him all his savings. What is more, he offers to accompany Orlando on his aimless, unprofitable journey.

Orlando is a noble-hearted young man. He knows how to value this loyalty as it should be valued. Adam has been in the family since he was a boy of seventeen and now he is an old man of eighty. Orlando gives him the love and respect that should be given to such a person.

When, on their journey, he becomes tired and cannot walk any further, Adam does not detain Orlando. Instead he tells him to go away, leaving him to his fate, for he does not want to be a burden to Orlando. This is true and selfless love. There are very few characters who can be at all compared with him. The Duke of Kent in *King Lear* is a nobleman, far above Adam in every way, but in selfless devotion to their masters the two can be put on the same level.

(viii) Touchstone

This is one of those figures that Shakespeare has added to the play, for there is no such character in Lodge's romance. He is one of the well-known jesters of Shakespeare. There are three of them who have become famous for their wit and wisdom: Touchstone, Feste in *Twelfth Night* and Fool in *King Lear*.

Fools or Jesters were well-known figures in Elizabethan drama. Most of the time they serve as witty entertainers and little more. It is in Shakespeare that we have the wise and subtle fool. It has been pointed out that Robert Armin joined Shakespeare's company at this time and he was a man of many accomplishments. He inspired the poet to create these well-known characters. M.C. Bradbrook says:

> The new feature about these parts is that they are dramatically interwoven with the central character and the central feeling of the play, they demand an actor ready to play many parts, not just his own brand of clowning.[16]

Touchstone is not of so high a standard as Feste or Lear's Fool, but he is definitely much more refined than his predecessors. It is to be noted that the two princesses select him, out of the entire court, to accompany them when they set out for the forest of Arden.

Wit and a talent for repartee are the stock-in-trade of a jester, and Touchstone has both. He, in many ways, is rather like Feste. When he enters the stage he proves a proposition in a logical manner (that a knight is forsworn) in the same way that Feste proves Olivia is a fool when he comes first on the stage. But he is not as highly accomplished as Feste is, for Feste is a good singer and can play on the tabor as well. Touchstone is not an equally good singer though he does sing a comic song in Act III, sc. iii.

There was a tradition of presenting a country fool and a town fool. In this play Touchstone has been contrasted with William, the country fool. Yet there is a difference. Touchstone is not really a fool in the sense of being stupid—he is a fool in a different sense—a jester, and a witty jester at that. It is not surprising, therefore, that he is able to win Audrey away from William who is a fool in the sense of being a stupid countryman, a bumpkin. Touchstone is fully aware of his own superiority over William:

> It is meat and drink to me to see a clown. By my troth, we that have good wits have much to answer for, we shall be flouting; we cannot hold.[17]

It is surprising, however, that he should choose Audrey for his mate, for she is a very simple village girl, with no trace of refinement about her. As he tells the Duke, it is a whimsy of his "to take that no man else will." He proves his own wit and courtly sophistication in this scene (Act V, sc. iv, ll. 38-100, pp. 86-87) when he engages in expounding to the Duke all the different kinds of lies and quips. These speeches are in the best tradition of Elizabethan fooling in which a fool is expected to be entertaining as well as witty, yet having an element of nonsense withal. This part of the scene whiles away the time as Rosalind and Celia change their dresses backstage. It should be kept in mind that the other such time-filling device he had used in this play occurs in Act II, sc. viii when the famous set-piece "All the world" was declaimed by Jaques. That speech is one of the best blank verse passages in Shakespeare and here Touchstone's two speeches, in their own sphere (prose passage of fooling) are equally representative of artistry in a different field.

(ix) Sir Oliver Martext

This character makes only one brief appearance and is a caricature of a pedantic village priest. He comes in Act II, sc. iii, in which Touchstone and Audrey plan to get married. They ask him to marry them and the first thing he asks is whether there is any one to give away the bride. Until there is someone to do this essential work he cannot marry the lovers. Then Jaques butts in and in the end manages to persuade Touchstone to seek out a better priest. When they go away Sir Oliver, undaunted, declares that such fools will not make him deviate from his duty. In other words he is a hidebound person, a stickler for rules. His personality, however, comes successfully across to us. He is one of the rare humour characters created by Shakespeare. It is rare for humour characters to rise above their humours and come across as a person, but Shakespeare has performed this feat with even a minor character like this.

(x) Corin

Corin the wise old shepherd is the counterpart of Silvius the young impetuous lover. Just as in pastoral literature there is a tradition of lovelorn young shepherds, so is there an equally strong tradition of the wise old shepherd who has obtained his wisdom from Mother Nature.

He is a tolerant old man who knows that the young lover's pangs of love will pass—he has passed through them himself. He also knows that no amount of advice will have any effect on Silvius's madness while he is still in the clutches of love. So he does not preach a homily, though he tries to hint that this experience is neither unique nor enduring.

When he sees Rosalind and Celia, he is extremely helpful. He helps them to settle in by buying the cottage and a flock of sheep for them. Later, in a dialogue with Touchstone he contrasts pastoral life with courtly life and utters one of the well-known speeches of this play:

> Sir, I am a true labourer. I earn that I eat, get that I wear, owe no man hate, envy no man's happiness, glad of other men's goods, content with my harm; and the greatest of my pride is to see my ewes graze and my lambs suck.[18]

He refuses to be irritated by Touchstone and attempts to annoy him and is too canny to be taken in by his wit. He is a man who knows that the life of a shepherd is not as idealistic as it looks from outside, but involves back-breaking work. Shakespeare has given the two traditional types of Shepherds in the two characters—Corin and Silvius, in the most concrete and credible manner possible.

(xi) Silvius

In Silvius we meet the kind of shepherd idealized in pastoral poetry—lovelorn young man scorned by his beloved. He is so true to type that he is almost a caricature. Indeed, he has been called a satirical portrayal of a traditional shepherd by those critics who look upon the theme of the pastoral as a satire.

Silvius loves Phoebe who scorns him and like all lovers thinks his experience to be unique. He hardly hears Corin telling him that he too had been equally intensely in love when he was young. He is far too wrapped up in himself, which again, is quite natural. He pleads with Phoebe and is not discouraged by her refusals. He is so blindly in love that he does not perceive it when she falls in love with Rosalind-Ganymede and gladly agrees to carry her letter to the latter.

When he does give the letter to Rosalind and she reads it out to him, he realizes that it is a love-letter and is yet not shaken in his loyalty. Rosalind understands that he cannot stop loving Phoebe and is ready to have her on any terms. She decides, therefore, that he really should be married to Phoebe for, as no one knows better than herself, Phoebe's love for herself as Ganymede is a mirage so, in the end, Silvius has his heart's desire just as Orlando, Oliver and Touchstone do.

As has been pointed out earlier, Silvius has to be contrasted with Corin as the portrayal of one example of the traditional shepherd as Corin is the portrayal of another type. In his aspect of a lover he can be equally well compared with Orlando who represents the Petrarchan courtly lover. In his case, however, he is the rejected lover whereas the hero is the successful one.

(xii) Celia

We now come to the minor female characters and Celia is the most important of them. She is Rosalind's cousin and the two of them love each other so much that they cannot live without each other. So when Duke Senior leaves for the forest of Arden Rosalind stays with Celia.

How strong and sincere her love for Rosalind is becomes clear when Rosalind is banished. First of all, Celia tries to plead for Rosalind. Then, when banishment becomes inevitable she quietly takes the decision of accompanying Rosalind. The latter is so stunned by this unexpected blow of fate that she can hardly react to it. Celia, therefore, sees that it is for her to take the initiative and she has the ability to do so. It is she who suggests that they should go to the forest of Arden to seek out her uncle and Rosalind's father, Duke Senior. Then she suggests that they should go in disguise. By this time Rosalind has recovered and enters into the spirit of the thing, but the first step is taken by Celia. She it is who suggests where they should go, and how.

In her decision to accompany Rosalind, the dramatist has departed a little from his source. In Lodge *Rosalynde* Alinda (who is Celia's counterpart) is banished by her father Torismond.

Here the whole event is made far more credible by making it a voluntary self-sacrifice:

> Here we may at first glance feel that Shakespeare's action is more plausible...and yet again Shakespeare's action is more mysterious, more wonderful, for devotion of such magnitude is inexplicable.[19]

It is not actually inexplicable, for Celia loves her cousin and one can do anything for the person one loves. Shakespeare has shown insight into this affectionate nature of Celia—she is blessed with a nature that is capable of intense, selfless love.

Later in the play there is another example of her capacity to love. This comes to light when she meets Oliver. It is a case of love at first sight. As has been already pointed out, there are three such examples of love at first sight in the play and this is the third. Oliver and Celia make up, in order of time, the fourth pair of lovers in the play. This love of theirs has been called one of the improbabilities of the play. Celia's quiet yet strong nature is, however, quite capable of lending itself to a deep and enduring passion generated at the very first sight of the loved one.

(xiii) Phoebe

Phoebe the shepherdess is the typical disdainful shepherdess of pastoral poetry, just as Silvius is the typical lovelorn shepherd. She is pursued by Silvius but is herself unmoved. Though she tries to rebuff and discourage Silvius, his infatuation is such that nothing she says has any effect.

Then a transformation comes over her, as Rosalind chides her after she has rebuffed her lover. Rosalind, very indignant, is cruelly frank with her, telling her that she has nothing to recommend her—she is a very ordinary girl and should be thankful that Silvius loves her. Instead of being offended at this scolding from a total stranger, Phoebe falls in love with one whom she takes for a very handsome young man. After giving her a piece of her mind Rosalind walks off and Phoebe quotes the famous line of Marlowe:

> Dead Shepherd, now I find thy saw of might,
> "Who ever loved that loved not at first-sight?"[20]

Then Shakespeare presents her in a most unattractive light, for she exploits the unquestioning devotion of Silvius in order to send a love-letter to Rosalind-Ganymede. She makes a fool of him by saying that she is going to write an insulting letter to Rosalind and he accepts whatever she says. She shows herself to be a truly heartless and unscrupulous person over this affair.

Later she comes and accuses Rosalind of having betrayed her to Silvius. Then in the dialogue that follows she affirms her love for Ganymede repeatedly and finally promises that if she, on the next day, refuses to marry this hypothetical young man then she will marry Silvius.

This is exactly what happens the next day, for she realizes that her beloved Ganymede is actually a princess. The only good action she does in the entire play is to accept her discomfiture gracefully and remain true to her promise. First, on seeing Ganymede as Rosalind she exclaims:

> If sight and shape be true,
> Why then, my love, adieu![21]

Then, after Hymen has joined the lovers, each pair separately, in marriage, she turns to Silvius, now her husband, and says:

> I will not eat my word, now thou art mine
> Thy faith my fancy to thee doth combine.[22]

It is doubtful how seriously Shakespeare had meant this shepherd couple to be taken. The two of them make up an essential part of the pastoral environment though Shakespeare has made Phoebe a ridiculous figure by making her fall in love with Rosalind.

Apart from these, there are a few more minor characters like Dennis (Oliver's servant), William the rejected lover of Audrey, and the goat-girl Audrey herself. There are also the two First Lords of Duke Senior's retinue and Frederick's court respectively. Shakespeare has given individuality to each of them though they come on the stage for a very short time.

REFERENCES

1. Act I, sc. iii, l. 58, p. 19.
2. Act V, sc. iv, ll. 157-59, p. 90.

3. Act I, sc. ii, ll. 254-55, p. 16.
4. Act I, sc. ii, ll. 265-71, p. 17.
5. Barnet, S., *op. cit.*, p. 180.
6. Act II, sc. i, ll. 18-20, p. 22.
7. Act II, sc. v, ll. 1-5, p. 31.
8. Act II, sc. iii, ll. 174-76, p. 39.
9. Act I, sc. ii, ll. 254-55, p. 16.
10. Act I, sc. i, l. 259, p. 16.
11. Act I, sc. i, ll. 109-13, p. 6.
12. Act IV, sc. iii, ll. 135-37, p. 75.
13. Quoted in Brown, J.R., *op. cit.*, p. 177.
14. Act V, sc. iv, ll. 157-62, p. 90.
15. Act I, sc. i, ll. 79-80, p. 5.
16. Palmer, D.J., ed., *Twelfth Night: A Casebook*, Macmillan, 1979, p. 223.
17. Act V, sc. i, ll. 10-12, p. 77.
18. Act III, sc. ii, ll. 71-75, p. 43.
19. Barnet, Sylvan, *op. cit.*, p. 174.
20. Act III, sc. v, ll. 81-82, p. 61.
21. Act V, sc. iv, ll. 117-18, p. 88.
22. Act V, sc. iv, ll. 146-47, p. 89.

8

The Plot-Structure

Aristotle has given six elements for tragedy, and plot is the first and most important of them. He calls it "the soul of tragedy." The loss of the second book of *Poetics* dealing with comedy poses some problems in knowing his views on comedy, but it should be kept in mind that based on some basic principles, the rules he has given in *Poetics* apply, not just to tragedy, but almost to all kinds of plays. Comedies, of course, end happily whereas tragedies end unhappily. In addition, comedies usually have a more complex structure, with intrigues and episodes in greater number than tragedies have. The rules concerning plots have been handed down by generations of classical scholars led by Aristotle and were known to the Elizabethans. Some of the basic rules shall be discussed, and their relevance for *As You Like It*.

THE CLASSICAL RULES AND AS YOU LIKE IT

The Unities: The so-called rules of the three unities, the unity of action, unity of time and of place, generally attributed to Aristotle, came to England mainly through the writings of the critics of the Italian Renaissance: Scaliger, Minturno, Castelvetro *et al.* Aristotle talks mainly of the unity of action and only incidentally about the unity of time. He does not say anything at all about the unity of place. It was due to the misreading of Aristotle by the Italian critics that the unity of place was also regarded as one of the Aristotelian unities. However, these rules have become famous and are applied to all kinds of plays. It is a well-known fact that Shakespeare did not pay much attention to these rules, and violates them with impunity in most of the plays, though *The Tempest* is an exception.

(a) **The Unity of Action:** This rule holds that there should not be any mixing of serious and comic actions. Though this rule is specially important for tragedies, it is applied to comedies also. A comedy should not have serious and tragic actions. Such actions produce pity and terror, and these have been relegated to tragedies. Comedies should have actions that produce laughter. Such a rule is more relevant for satirical comedies, but it applies to other kinds of comedies as well.

Many of Shakespeare's comedies contain serious actions, but this is not the case with the present play. There is nothing that mars its mood of serenity and happiness. This had been pointed out by Dowden:

> No real adversity has come to any of them. Shakespeare, when he put into the Duke's mouth the words "Sweet are the uses of adversity" knew something of deeper affliction than a life in the golden leisure of Arden. Of real melancholy there is none in the play.[1]

(b) The Unity of Time: According to Aristotle, the action of a play should cover the time-span of "a single revolution of the sun," or a full day. In the strictest sense the unity of time means that the action of a play should cover only as much time as is taken by the actual performance. In other words, if the story of a play takes two hours on the stage then the actual time covered by the story should also take two hours. This seems to be impossible, but this is the case with classical tragedies. Aristotle's theory of one full day, too, is quite difficult, but not outside the bounds of possibility. Ben Jonson's plays take one full day, from morning till evening.

This time-scheme, however, is not possible to observe in all kinds of plays—the chronicle plays, for example. Shakespeare hardly ever observes this rule (except in *The Tempest*). The most well-known, or notorious, violation of this rule is to be found in the *The Winter's Tale* where an interval of sixteen years occurs within the play. So far as the play under discussion is concerned, it is not sure how long a span of time has been covered. Definitely, the action takes a few months, for though in the beginning there is clear indication that the first and the second scenes take place on two consecutive days, the third might come a few days later. After that, Orlando, Adam and the two princesses must have spent at least a day or perhaps a few days to reach the forest. As to how many days or weeks are spent there, no one can be sure but a few months must have elapsed for when Oliver at last reaches the forest he is "a wretched ragged man/O'ergrown with hair."[2] It must have taken him three or four months at least to grow so much hair. It can therefore be concluded that a time-span of quite a few months must be covered by the play.

(c) **The Unity of Place:** This rule demands that there should be no changes of scenes in a play. The action should take place in one place only. Sophocles's *Oedipus Rex* for example, takes place in the audience-chamber of King Oedipus. Among the Elizabethans, Ben Jonson had kept this rule in mind, though he too, gives a few changes of scenes.

Shakespeare had not paid much attention to this rule either. Not only different places in the same city, but different countries are covered in his plays. Though neo-classical critics had roundly condemned him for not observing the rules, Dr. Johnson's defence, particularly for the violation of this rule, has become famous. In *As You Like It* many different places provide the location: Oliver's house and the adjoining orchard, Duke Frederick's palace and the open meadow outside the palace, the outskirts of the forest and the forest itself. Thus, there are several changes of scenes. No stickler for rules, Shakespeare has not limited the locations of his scenes within a constricted area.

Many other rules about plot were laid down by Aristotle. Later commentators explained and added to these. It is a well-known fact that Latin works were more popular in Elizabethan times than Greek. One such writer was Donatus, whose work was part of the school curriculum in those days. In this treatise Donatus explains the several parts of a play. According to him the Prologue is the first part of the play. It is a short speech, coming before the actual action begins, telling the reader about the theme and the story of the play. There are several plays of Shakespeare that have such a Prologue attached to them. Usually, however (as, indeed, is the case with most of the other playwrights of his time), he incorporates the Prologue within the first scene of the play. This is the case with the present play, which does not have a Prologue. Instead it has the expository dialogue in the first scene in which Orlando's position in his brother's household, and sundry other matters, are told to us.

Besides these particulars about the plot, there were some other classical features that were known and used by Elizabethan dramatists. One such device is "Peripeteia" or Reversal of fortune. This term is usually used with reference to tragic heroes whose fortunes undergo a change for the worse, and therefore the term has a negative association. With reference to comedy, however, it can take on a positive colouring for it can then mean a change from adversity to prosperity. There are many of such reversals in our play. Orlando and Rosalind are both forced to leave their homes and wander shelterless. Later the same happens to Oliver. When these characters reach the forest they have peace for some time, but prosperity has not come yet. True prosperity comes only at the end, with Duke Frederick's renunciation, but this reversal is not actually shown in the play.

Another important element of the plot, which also involves characters, is that of Recognition or *Anagnorisis*. This can be of a very simple kind as when characters who have been separated meet and recognize each other. The Recognition-scene in *Twelfth Night* is an example of this kind of recognition. The most subtle kind of recognition is self-recognition, in which a character is able to recognize the complexities hidden within himself.

There are three recognitions, all of a very simple variety, to be found in this play. The Duke and Orlando, both recognize Rosalind:

Duke: If there be truth in sight, you are my daughter.

Orlando: If there be truth in sight, you are my Rosalind.[3]

The third recognition is that of Phoebe's who recognizes Rosalind as the shepherd Ganymede:

If sight and shape be true
Why, then, my love, adieu.[4]

This is slightly more complex than the recognition of the Duke and Orlando, both of whom had known Rosalind and can identify her as such. Phoebe, however, had not known her as Rosalind. She had known her only as Ganymede. So her recognition is a negative recognition for she knows Rosalind as not-Ganymede. The Duke's and Orlando's are positive recognition for they know her as Rosalind as she was before she had adopted disguise.

There is another well-known device used in comedies known as the *deus ex machina*. When the plot reaches complications of such proportions that it cannot be easily disentangled, the dramatist makes use of this device. It means "god from a machine." In classical plays a heavenly figure like Zeus, Apollo or someone like them, would be brought on the stage and iron out all difficulties with his heavenly power so that the play may end happily. In English an authoritative, powerful figure, like that of the king, usually takes on this function. Aristotle (and others) is not much in favour of this device but it has been widely used. In the present play Jaques de Boys performs the function of a *deus ex machina* when he comes at the end to announce that the kingdom of Duke Senior has been resorted to him. The plot, by this time, has already reached the desired end of a romantic comedy, the marriage of four couples, and this message completes the happiness of everyone concerned. It is a very successful use of this device.

CERTAIN ELIZABETHAN FEATURES IN *AS YOU LIKE IT*

There are certain features peculiar to Elizabethan drama that shall now be discussed. First of all, all these plays are double-or-multiple plotted. Aristotle was not in favour of more than one plot in a play, and the Old Classical Comedies are single-plotted. Innovations, however, were made as the New Classical Comedy developed and, often enough, one comes across multiple-plotted plays. The Elizabethans developed theirs after these later models, particularly those of Plautus and Terence. Ben Jonson who was an admirer of Terence, made all his comedies at least double-plotted and most often multiple-plotted. This is the case with our poet also. Shakespeare's plays are usually double-plotted, having one main plot and one sub-plot. In *As You Like It*, we have a multiple-plotted play. In the main plot there are Rosalind and Orlando who are forced to flee their own homes and seek refuge elsewhere. Duke Senior with his courtiers makes up one of the sub-plots. Here there is some difference in critical opinions, for some include it within the main plot. We have another sub-plot a pastoral one, in Silvius and Phoebe and a fourth in Touchstone-Audrey-William. Thus, the play is a multiple-plotted comedy, with characters from different classes coming together and interacting.

The use of masques in plays is an Elizabethan custom that Shakespeare uses many times in his plays. The masque of Hymen in *As You Like It* is one of the examples of his use of this popular contemporary convention. It is a brief musical play-within-the-play involving supernatural characters (as in this play), personifications of different aspects of nature like seasons, etc. Masques can be very simple, as the one in *As You Like It*, or quite elaborate mini-plays as the one in *The Tempest*.

The masque was a very popular form of entertainment at Court and in the castles of noblemen. Ben Jonson wrote many masques for the Queen's entertainment in which the courtiers themselves took part. The first of such independent masques (i.e., not belonging to a play) was the *Masque of Blackness* by Ben Jonson in collaboration with Inigo Jones, who designed the sets, in 1605. Thereafter, the masque became very popular for it provided music as well as spectacle, two of the essentials of drama as given by Aristotle. As B. Blackstone remarks:

> It was a sort of embryonic opera, treating of mythological and allegorical subjects, in which music, dance and elaborate décor existed on equal terms with poetry.[5]

Shakespeare has made use of this colourful and highly appealing form of entertainment in order to celebrate the multiple weddings in this play. (*Vide* Ch. 4, *supra* and Ch. 10, *infra*, for further details.)

Another popular stage-convention of the time was the use of disguises. This device is used to lend the play complexity, surprise, dramatic irony or tension. Shakespeare excelled in the use of disguises, particularly that of the heroine:

> ...his most constant and successful use is that of the page's doublet and hose for the heroine.[6]

Such disguises were quite convenient because in those days female roles were enacted by young boys. The longer the character was in disguise the longer the freedom for the boy-actor. There is a lot of complexity involved here. The audience knows that it is a boy who is playing the role and so when the character dons a disguise things become more complex. M.C. Bradbrook looks upon the use of disguise with approval—it

> enlarges the original role, and also discovers its latent possibilities.[7]

In this play Rosalind and Celia both disguise themselves for a considerable length of time. We see them in their own selves in two scenes (Act I, sc. ii and iii) and after that in the second part of the last scene. For the major part of the play Rosalind is Ganymede and Celia is Aliena. It is particularly Rosalind's disguise that is the most significant as well as the most entertaining aspect of the play. It adds to the dramatic irony of the play as well as a double vision in which, in certain scenes the single figure of Rosalind is seen simultaneously as Ganymede and as Rosalind by Orlando. Referring to this feature, John Russell Brown has pointed out that it adds a special dimension and intensification to the plot:

> Within the predominantly wide focus of the comedy, a double vision gives a kind of flickering intensity and during a few moments of avowal, ...the dramatic focus may be still, deep and intimate.[8]

The phrase "double vision" or "enlargement" is not enough to explain the extent of complexity in Rosalind's disguise, particularly in the love-game scene (Act IV, sc. i). Several levels of perception are present here. Put in a systematic manner thus:

Orlando knows only one level: Ganymede pretends to be Rosalind.

Celia knows two: (i) Rosalind disguised as Ganymede and (ii) Ganymede pretends to be Rosalind.

The audience knows three levels: (i) the boy enacting the role of Rosalind, (ii) Rosalind disguised as Ganymede, and (iii) Ganymede pretending to be Rosalind.

Thus for the audience or the reader the situation achieves the maximum of complexity. No less than four personalities are involved: the boy-actor, the actual Rosalind, the disguised Rosalind-Ganymede, and finally the Rosalind that Ganymede pretends to be. Shakespeare, however, executes his task of putting all this across with great aplomb.

The Sources of *As You Like It*

The Elizabethan-Jacobean dramatists mostly took the material for their plays from a large number of literary works already in existence. Narrative poems, prose romances, histories, old plays—all were grist to their mills. The study of Shakespeare's sources, his treatment of them, etc. has become an important branch of Shakespeare studies. It is fascinating to see how he selects his material from half a dozen or more sources, rejects some, retains some, expands some and contracts some in order to fulfill his artistic needs.

The chief sources for *As You Like It* were the prose romance *Rosalynde* or *Euphues' Golden Legacy* by Lodge and another play *Sir Clyomon and Clamydes*, and a narrative poem *Tale of Gamelyn*. Lodge himself has based his romance on this last one expanding it in many ways. Our poet in his turn took the basic story but altered it in many different ways. The most important of these alterations are as follows:

1. In Lodge the brothers quarrel long after the wrestling-match.

   In Shakespeare the quarrel takes place immediately before the match.

2. Rosader (Orlando's counterpart in Lodge) stays for some time with Saladyne (the counterpart of Oliver) after the wrestling and Rosalynde too is banished some time later, thought it is not clear how long.

In Shakespeare Orlando's departure and Rosalind's banishment occur just after the match.

3. In Lodge Rosader is chained by his brother and is released by Adam.

   Shakespeare omits this.

4. In Lodge Alinda is kidnapped by bandits and rescued by Saladyne.

   Shakespeare omits this.

5. Lodge's romance ends with a battle.

   In Shakespeare the play ends with the renunciation of Frederick and marriages.

6. Shakespeare introduces four new persons,—Jaques, Touchstone, Audrey and William.

Apart from these there are numerous minor changes. For example when in Lodge Rosalynde and Aliena (in Shakespeare they have Touchstone with them) reach the forest after many days they do not meet anyone (in Shakespeare they meet Corin and buy the cottage etc. from him). Instead they see Montanus' (the counterpart of Silvius) poem hanging from the boles of the trees. Then they walk on and meet two shepherds in the evening. There are numerous changes like these, some of which have already been pointed out. As Bullough has observed:

> His play is more than an adaptation of Lodge's romance, but it must already be obvious that he drew much from it, both in detail and for his general concept.[9]

The Plot of *As You Like It*

As You Like It is not a double-plotted play, but a multiple-plotted one, involving different social classes and totally different environments. It has been interpreted in many different ways for example: court versus country life, pastoral versus romance, fortune versus nature, etc. These different interpretations highlight the complexity of the plot.

The main plot, of course, is that of the two lovers, Rosalind and Orlando. Rosalind is the victim of fortune because her father, Duke Senior, has been betrayed by his own brother and driven out of his kingdom. Rosalind has not accompanied him but remains in the palace, as her uncle the usurper has a daughter and the two cousins are devoted to each other.

Then Rosalind meets Orlando and the two fall deeply in love with each other. Orlando's life is made miserable by his elder brother who is actively hostile to him and plots his death. Orlando escapes from one such plot (a wrestling-match in which the rival wrestler is hinted by Oliver to maim or kill Orlando) and is warned in time to escape another. He and his devoted servant leave their home and set forth on an aimless journey which ends when they reach the forest of Arden where Duke Senior has taken refuge.

Rosalind is suddenly banished from the kingdom by her uncle. She and her cousin Celia disguise themselves as a shepherd and a shepherdess respectively and set out for the forest of Arden, accompanied by Touchstone the jester.

Rosalind and Orlando meet in the forest. Here they have an elaborate game of love in which Rosalind, still disguised as the shepherd-boy called Ganymede, pretends to be Rosalind and is courted by Orlando. Finally, after some time (perhaps a few weeks, perhaps a few months) she reveals her own identity and Celia's and is happily married to Orlando.

The wrestling-match, the love-game, the meeting between Oliver and Celia are all intrigues or episodes within this main plot.

Duke Senior with the loyal lords who have accompanied him in his exile make up one of the sub-plots. It has been suggested that this should be treated as part of the main plot and not a sub-plot in its own as the characters belong to the same aristocratic level. Different critics think differently.

Here we have the Duke who has been foully betrayed by his own younger brother Frederick and has had to flee his kingdom and seek refuge in the forest of Arden. Here they lead a carefree and happy life, for though Nature is cruel at times, she is a bountiful and benevolent goddess. Orlando comes to him and is welcomed into his group. Then comes the day when Rosalind-Ganymede reveals her own identity and that of Celia and are joyfully accepted by the Duke. He willingly gives her in marriage to Orlando. At the end of the play his kingdom is restored to him.

Next there is the pastoral sub-plot of the shepherd couple Silvius and Phoebe. Both of them are stock figures taken out of traditional pastoral eclogues. Silvius is deeply in love with Phoebe, but Phoebe rejects him. Then Phoebe meets Rosalind disguised as Ganymede and at once falls in love with her. Thus a love-triangle Ganymede-Silvius-Phoebe is formed and tension is created. All these problems are solved when Rosalind puts off her disguise and Silvius and Phoebe are joined in marriage, for Phoebe had been made to promise to do so the previous day.

Another sub-plot is that of Touchstone and Audrey. Touchstone the jester is attracted towards the goat-girl Audrey and the two decide to marry. Here also there is a love-triangle because William the village yokel loves Audrey who rejects him and turns to Touchstone. The two are joined in marriage.

All these different plots are intricately woven with each other. Orlando of the main plot meets and is accepted by Duke Senior within his group. Rosalind of the main plot generates love in the heart of Phoebe of the other sub-plot. Touchstone, who rightfully belongs to the main plot falls in love with Audrey, making up a different sub-plot. This constant interaction among the characters of the different plots gives the play great complexity and richness. A brief scene-wise chart of the action and locations used in the play will make this highly complex interweaving clear:

Act I, sc. i — Oliver's house. Orlando and Oliver quarrel.

sc. ii — Duke Frederick's lawn. The wrestling-match takes place. Rosalind and Orlando fall in love with each other.

sc. iii — Rosalind is banished.

Act II, sc. i — The forest of Arden. Duke Senior's life therein presented.

sc. ii — Frederick discovers the flight of his own daughter with Rosalind.

sc. iii — Orlando is warned and flees with Adam.

sc. iv —	Rosalind, Celia and Touchstone reach the forest of Arden.
sc. v —	The courtiers of Duke Senior presented.
sc. vi —	Orlando and Adam reach the forest.
sc. vii —	Orlando interrupts Duke Senior's feast. He is welcomed into the group.
Act III, sc. i —	Duke Frederick banishes Oliver.
sc. ii —	Orlando and Rosalind-Ganymede meet. They decide to play the love-game.
sc. iii —	Touchstone and Audrey decide to marry. Jaques from the Duke-plot meets them.
sc. iv —	Dialogue between Rosalind and Celia.
sc. v —	Phoebe rejects Silvius. She is reprimanded by Rosalind-Ganymede and falls in love with her. Love-triangle formed.
Act IV, sc. i —	Rosalind and Orlando play the love-game.
sc. ii —	The hunting-scene with the followers of Duke Senior.
sc. iii —	Silvius of the pastoral sub-plot gives Phoebe's love-letter to Rosalind. Oliver comes and relates how Orlando saved his life and how his own heart has undergone a total change.
Act V, sc. i —	Touchstone, Audrey and William meet.
sc. ii —	Oliver tells Orlando of his impending marriage. Rosalind promises Orlando that he shall marry Rosalind the next day. She makes Phoebe promise to marry Silvius if she refuses to marry Ganymede.
sc. iii —	Two of the Duke's pages sing a song.
sc. iv —	Rosalind and Celia reveal their identities. A Masque in which Hymen joins the four pairs of lovers in marriage. Jaques de Boys announces the conversion of Frederick and the restoration of his kingdom to Duke Senior.
Epilogue —	Spoken by Rosalind.

This synopsis shows how, with great artistry, Shakespeare alternates the scenes among the different groups of characters, thus weaving the different strands of the plots strongly together.

The five-Act structure followed by Shakespeare and others accommodated many of the elements of classical plays, though not all of them. For example, there is no Prologue to this play. Usually, if there is no Prologue the first scene takes on the function of the Prologue and that is what has happened here. The first scene between the two brothers is almost entirely expository in nature as is also the dialogue between Orlando and Adam in the beginning of it. We are told, as in a classical prologue, all that had happened before the opening of the play: how Sir Rowland de Boys had left his property, what provisions he had made for Orlando etc. We are also told how Duke Senior has been banished and has gone to the forest of Arden, leaving his only daughter behind. Herein the first scene fulfills the functions of a prologue. Bullough, commenting on this feature, points out:

> Shakespeare begins *in medias res* with Orlando's complaints, his quarrel with Oliver and the arrival of the wrestler.[10]

It has to be noted that though Shakespeare begins *in medias res* he does not go back to the beginning as is often done with such techniques. His play goes forward and onwards.

Then, as the play proceeds, the different strands of the different plots are taken up in different scenes. The dramatist keeps a firm hold on the story and though there are different plots with different sets of characters from different spheres of society, no bewilderment is caused, nor is there any excessive complexity. *Peripeteia* and *anagnorisis*, the two important ingredients of plot are cleverly interwoven. *Peripeteia* comes to no less than three characters, not counting Duke Senior. Orlando is driven from home, Rosalind is banished and Oliver's property is confiscated and he himself driven out. *Anagnorisis* comes at the end of the play when Duke Senior and Orlando recognize Rosalind and Celia. In this scene *peripeteia*, in an inverted sense, is at work again, this time bringing happiness and prosperity as the fortunes of the chief characters undergo a change for the better and the happy interlude in the forest comes to an end.

The last stage of the plot, the Epilogue, is present in the play. Many plays of Shakespeare have epilogues, but none is spoken by a female character. Here Rosalind delivers the Epilogue and makes it clear that the play is a light-hearted one.

In spite of a neat ending, the plot of this play has been adversely criticized. It has been observed that Shakespeare has not spent enough care and artistry over the first part of the play as he is in too much of a hurry to bring all the chief characters to the forest of Arden:

> In *As You Like It* the plot is handled in the most perfunctory way. Shakespeare crams his first Act with incidents in order to get everyone to the forest as soon as he possibly can.[11]

Another feature of the plot that many critics have objected to is the presence of so many improbabilities in it. The sudden love of Rosalind and Orlando for example and the equally sudden love of Oliver and Celia for each other, Frederick's sudden banishment of Rosalind, Celia's determination to accompany her, Oliver's sudden change of heart and Frederick's equally sudden religious conversion—these have offended the critics. These features have all been discussed when these different characters have been analysed (*vide* Chs. 6 and 7, *supra*). None of them is incredible or impossible and some (e.g. the sudden springing of love in the heart) are based solidly on literary tradition as well as stage conventions.

The plot has been interpreted in quite a few ways. Sherman, Hawkins looks at the play as a "green world comedy" (*vide* Ch. 3, *supra*) and interprets the plot from this point of view:

> In green-world comedy the hero and the heroine begin by leaving the old world behind them: whether they are exiled or elope or set off to seek their fortunes, the first phase of the action is an exodus.[12]

The next part of the action usually takes place in the green world where the hero and the heroine take refuge. There are many obstacles in the way of their union. Hawkins, however, does not trace in detail the development of the plot in accordance with this theory.

This is but one theory about the plot of *As You Like It*. There are many such. The diligent student will find that all these theories add to our understanding of the play.

REFERENCES

1. Dowden, E., *op. cit.*, p. 36.
2. Act IV, sc. iii, l. 106, p. 74.
3. Act V, sc. iv, ll. 115-16, p. 88.
4. Act V, sc. iv, ll. 117-18, p. 88.
5. Blackstone, Bernard, *Shakespeare: The Tempest*, Notes on Literature series issued by the British Council, London, Feb. 1969, p. 7.
6. Bradbrook, M.C., *op. cit.*, p. 88.
7. *Ibid.*
8. Brown, John Russell, *op. cit.*, p. 81.
9. Bullough, *op. cit.*, p. 148.
10. *Ibid.*
11. Gardner, Helen, *op. cit.*, p. 153.
12. Hawkins, Sherman, *op. cit.*, p. 52.

9

Imagery in *As You Like It*

Images do not only serve to embellish poetry but also to make it more effective. This aspect of Shakespearean drama has been emphasized by the critics of modern times and has been studied in great detail. The development of his imagery from the beginning of his career to the last play, the function of his imagery, the complex relationship between his imagery and the theme of the play—all these have been carefully studied and analysed. Henri Fluchère has given a very good working definition of imagery:

> Imagery may shortly be defined as a concrete illustration drawn upon by the poet to clarify or embellish the object that he seeks to describe.[1]

Fluchère here talks about only two functions of imagery—embellishing and clarifying, but as far as Shakespeare is concerned, his imagery has some other functions as well. Anticipating future events, creating the atmosphere, expressing the mood of the character who is speaking—such are the functions carried out by Shakespeare's images.

A study of his imagery should also alert one to the fact that it is often impossible or at least very difficult, to distinguish between rhetorical figures, images and symbols. These three are integrally related and often overlapped. That is to say, an image can be studied as a figure of speech and quite often it might take on the status of a symbol as well. Pointing this characteristic out, Fluchère says:

> No strict rule allows us to say at what point we pass from the plane of pure rhetoric, to the plane of pure psychology, and even the metaphysical plane, in the use of imagery.[2]

Again, depending upon the method of categorization, the same image will come under different heads, i.e. a sense image will also be a nature image or a domestic image or some other kind. This, of course, is a universal feature.

The most obvious and elementary group of images are sense-images. These, corresponding to our five senses, are of five kinds. Images referring to our sense of vision are visual images. Those that pertain to hearing are auditory, to smell are olfactory, to touch are tactile images. These shall now be briefly mentioned with reference to the text. Sense-images also have another special feature. One image might refer to several different senses or the object being referred to might appeal to one sense, but the poet might describe it in terms of a different one. This technique is known as synaesthesia.

We shall now study the images that have been used in this play. As it is not possible to study in detail, only a few obvious examples will be taken in order to illustrate different kinds of images. The longest scene in the play is the one in which the hero and the heroine meet in the forest of Arden for the first time. It offers a great wealth of fine images and it shall be noted how effective they are.

Right in the beginning of the scene there is a fine sense-image. It is a visual image concerning the moon:

> And thou, thrice crowned queen of night, survey
> With thy chaste eye, from thy pale sphere above,
> Thy huntress' name that my full life doth sway.[3]

This image seems to be quite a simple one, but this simplicity is deceptive. First of all it is a visual image, but this visual image includes another within it. The moon, which is being seen by humans, is herself in her turn looking down and seeing the earth, in particular the name of Rosalind that Orlando has carved on the barks of trees. Moreover, it is an image which is, besides being a visual image, also a lunar image and involves both the earth and the sky, i.e. both the divine and the human.

It is pointed out above that many images are so integrally woven with figures of speech that it is difficult to separate the two. In the three lines quoted above, for example, we find an apostrophe, for the moon is being addressed directly, a personification as the moon is also the Goddess Diana and also a mythical allusion, for Diana is a goddess belonging to the Graeco-Roman pantheon.

There is the use of tactile image in the dialogue between Touchstone and Corin in this same scene. Corin says that the pelts of ewes are greasy, that their own hands are hard and covered with tar. Again, when he says that the hands of courtiers are perfumed he makes use of olfactory imagery. Later still Touchstone, parodying Orlando's verses makes use of gustatory and olfactory images:

> Sweetest nut hath sourest rind,
> Such a nut is Rosalind
> He that sweetest rose will find
> Must find love's prick with Rosalind.[4]

Here, along with a gustatory image we also have the image of a fruit and in the second couplet, again, olfactory image goes hand in hand with a floral one. There is, however, nothing remarkable in this kind of blend of sense-images with images based on some other aspect of nature or life. Sense-images depend on some object perceived by our senses. Conversely, any image based on any object will also refer to one or another of our senses.

Animal imagery is expected in a work portraying pastoral surroundings and Shakespeare does not disappoint us. The bulk of the animal imagery in this scene is concerned with sheep but other animals are also brought in. Images concerned with sheep are used, as is but natural, by Corin. Talking about the daily life of a shepherd and its effect on their hands he says that the courtly habit of shaking hands cannot be imitated by shepherds:

> we are still handling our ewes, and their fells you know are greasy.[5]

His is a simple unambitious life and, in order to make Touchstone understand this he says:

> the greatest of my pride is to see my ewes graze and my lambs suck.[6]

These and other images used by Corin, are not merely animal images, they are also images of a professional sort, for they describe the profession of shepherds. Clemen has mentioned how, as his artistry developed, Shakespeare showed relationship between the character of the speaker and the imagery he uses. The simplicity of Corin's mind, his whole-hearted devotion to his work, the purity of the life he leads, all are amply illustrated by these and other pastoral images that he uses. In contrast, Silvius does not use images of this kind. He too is a shepherd like Corin, but his images do not have any connection with shepherding.

Touchstone brings some more animal imagery in, referring to deer and cats:

> If a hart do lack a hind,
> Let him seek out Rosalind.
> If the cat will after kind,
> So be sure will Rosalind.[7]

Images have also been taken from several different spheres of life. Images concerned with different branches of pastoral life abound in the speeches of Corin who talks about how he tends his flock and even performs surgery on them. There is an image concerned with harvest used by the jester in his parody of Orlando's verses:

> They that reap must sheaf and bind
> Then to cart with Rosalind.[8]

Then Rosalind makes use of imagery concerned with gardening. She says she found the verses on a branch of one of the trees:

Ros: Peace, you dull fool! I found them on a tree.

Touchst: Truly, the tree yields bad fruit.

Ros: I'll graft it with you, and then I shall graft it with a medlar: then it will be the earliest fruit

> i'th' country: for you'll be rotten ere you be half
> ripe, and that's the right virtue of the medlar.[9]

This image is a fruit-image and also image about grafting which has to do with country life and both are appropriate for the kind of life they are leading.

Another important point should be noted as far as this particular image is concerned. This is an image about cultivating fruits, involving grafting and shows knowledge of the nature of a medlar. Such images, containing more than one reference to a particular work etc. have been called "image-complexes" by Caroline Spurgeon:

> The term "image-complex" is to indicate that Shakespeare, in his imagery, shows, as Miss Spurgeon has put it, a predilection for "certain classes of things, certain qualities in things and certain aspects of life."[10]

Here, therefore, we have an image-complex in which the one comprehensive, all-inclusive image of gardening has been used, with many references to it. "Tree", "graft", "fruit", "medlar", "half ripe", are all words related to this image-complex.

As the scene proceeds we have more and more variety in imagery. Rosalind, talking to Celia, uses religious imagery related to preaching:

> O most gentle pulpiter, what tedious homily of love have you wearied your parishioners withal.[11]

This image is specifically concerned with preaching and thus it is a religious image that deals with the practical aspect of a preacher's life. At the same time it is also an auditory image as well as a visual one, for one can see the priest and also hear him preaching.

After this Rosalind and Celia talk and we have a witty dialogue in which there is a pun on the word "feet" as well as the image of a lame man. They are talking of the verses Orlando has written. The lines do not scan properly and some have more feet than they ought to:

Ros: Some of them had in them more feet than the verses would bear.

Cel: That's no matter, the feet might bear the verses.

Ros: Ay, but the feet were lame and could not bear themselves without the verse, and therefore stood lamely in the verse.[12]

The term "feet" applies to prosodic units in a line of verse naturally demands a pun on it. Thus, we have here an image related to prosody (which is abstract) being given human attributes and so developing into a concrete image.

The next important image in the scene is used again by Rosalind. This time it is a gustatory image about wine. Celia is teasing her, telling her and yet not telling that she has already met Orlando. Rosalind then pleads:

> I would thou couldst stammer, that thou mightest pour this concealed man out of thy mouth, as wine comes out of a narrow-mouthed bottle; either too much at once, or none at all. I prithee take the cork out of thy mouth that I may drink thy tidings.[13]

This is a homely image, yet it has been developed through two long sentences. Shakespeare has not elaborated the image much, for it would not have been appropriate in the context. Rosalind is impatient, and a long, elaborate image would be out of place here. Had he given us the colour of the wine then it would have been a gustatory image in which the visual element is highlighted. If he had also mentioned the sound of wine falling into a cup then auditory quality would have been added to it. There is a great scope in the elaboration of such an image, but Shakespeare knew where to draw the line. Rosalind is in an impatient frame of mind and a long elaborate image would have been most unsuitable and unrealistic.

This image, though not very elaborate, has been developed in two sentences. Later, when Orlando comes in and he talks there is a remarkable image concerning time. First of all, time has been given human attributes, so we have an abstract idea presented in concrete terms. Secondly, Rosalind's fancy shows itself in a charming inventive mood. She says that time does not pass in the same way for everyone. It passes slowly for some and rapidly for others. Then, in four successive passages she illustrates these characters in five successive images. First of all she uses the image of a bride in order to show how Time passes for her:

> ...he trots hard with a young maid between the contract of the marriage and the day it is solemnized: if the interim be but a se'nnight, Time's pace is so hard that it seems the length of seven years.

Next she shows how Time "ambles" for a priest and also for a rich person:

> With a priest that lacks Latin and a rich man that hath not the gout: for the one sleeps easily because he cannot study, and the other lives merrily because he feels no pain.

These images have been developed a little further, for the sentence does not end here. Then Orlando asks her who are the persons with whom Time gallops, and Rosalind answers, in a witty manner:

> With a thief to the gallows, for though he go as softly as foot can fall, he thinks himself too soon there.

The last image is that of a lawyer, with whom Time stays still and does not move at all:

> Or: Who stays it still withal?
>
> Ros: With lawyers in the vacation: for they sleep between term and term, and then they perceive not how Times moves.[14]

This remarkable succession of five images to explain and illustrate but one idea is very rare, even in Shakespeare. Very often, in poetry, he piles image upon image but this kind of elaborate image (each developed in one sentence which is long and carefully formed) is rare in prose. So we have here, in a leisurely manner which is perfectly and realistically in keeping with the mood of the scene, five images illustrating one idea: that of a bride, a priest, a healthy rich man, a thief and a lawyer, spread out over no less than twenty lines. It is not at all surprising that Orlando should be highly impressed by this exhibition of wit in one whom he takes for a rustic, a shepherd.

Another such passage that provides a parallel to this succession of images to be found in this play itself, is Jaques's famous speech on the Seven Ages of Man. There also the central image is that of a human being and no less than seven fine and distinctive images have been given to describe human life in its entirety—from infancy to senility. Each of them has become famous. Indeed, this passage is one of the best passages of Shakespeare and can be analysed in many different ways.

As the play is primarily concerned with the intricacies of pastoral life, nature images abound in it. Shakespeare's wonderful ability to present nature images had been recognized by his early critics. Dryden, it is well-known, did not approve of the extraordinary world of Shakespearean imagery, but in spite of this he could not help but praise his nature images:

> All the images of nature were still present to him and he drew them, not laboriously, but luckily, when he describes anything, you more than see it, you feel it too.[15]

In this scene nature images are present from the very beginning. Thus, Orlando, hanging verses from the branches of trees says:

> O Rosalind! these trees shall be my books,
> And in their barks my thoughts I'll character.[16]

Orlando repeats this idea many times more in his poems thus giving a tree-image every time. This, again, is perfectly in tune, and indeed expected, in a play placed against a pastoral perspective. Such tree-images recur, not only in Orlando's speeches, but throughout the play in the speeches of the other characters as well. Amiens sings of the leisurely life "under the greenwood tree", Duke Senior finds "tongues in tree", his first Lord mentions an old Oak tree under which a wounded stag lay down—there are numerous such examples.

This kind of image, i.e. the same image occurring again and again throughout a work, has been designated as an "iterative image" by Caroline Spurgeon. Such images help create the proper atmosphere. Imagery thus ceases to be just decorative and becomes integral to the play.

This particular scene is not very rich in nature images, yet there are a few remarkable ones. Thus, referring to the manner in which, against all probabilities, Celia has met Orlando, she uses a nature-image:

> ...it is a hard matter for friends to meet, but mountains may be removed with earthquakes, and so encounter.[17]

This image is a striking one because here two ideas, opposed to each other, are juxtaposed. Mountains are entirely static, and earthquakes are dynamic, causing movement where there was no movement before. Mountains are the very symbols of surety and stability whereas earthquakes are symbols of destruction and instability. These opposing denotations are put side by side. Again all earthquakes have negative associations, but our poet has given an earthquake a positive value here, for it brings together separated persons.

The most memorable of the nature images in this play occur not in this scene, but in the two songs sung by Amiens. The first of them ("Under the greenwood tree") gives two images that describe the benevolent aspect of nature:

> Under the greenwood tree,
> Who loves to lie with me,
> And turn his merry note
> Unto the sweet bird's throat...[18]

Here the greenwood tree and the tuneful song-bird give the impression of happy spring-time beauty. The second stanza, in contrast, points out the cruel aspect of nature. Both of them create the pastoral atmosphere. According to Clemen, we have images that serve to beautify the style in the early plays of Shakespeare, but, as his art matured, gradually his images became more and more functional and integrally related to the play:

> The more Shakespeare becomes a conscious dramatic artist, the more he employs them for dramatic purposes.

> The images gradually lose their purely "poetic", often extraneous nature and become one of the dramatic elements.[19]

These images quoted above help create the pastoral atmosphere as also do those concerned with sheep used by Corin. Such images are not merely pretty pictures but are functional ones, integrated into the fabric of the play.

Accumulation of images is a typical and regularly recurring feature of Shakespeare's work. Very often they serve decorative purposes, specially in the early plays, and often they serve to highlight or emphasize certain ideas. This scene contains an extraordinary example of accumulated images in the parody that Touchstone makes up, on the spur of the moment, of Orlando's verses:

> If a hart do lack a hind,
> Let him seek out Rosalind:
> If the cat will after kind,
> So be sure will Rosalind:
> Winter garments must be lines,
> So must slender Rosalind
> They that reap must sheaf and bind
> Then to cart with Rosalind.[20]

The poem continues for two more couplets, each giving one image. Thus, we have a quick succession of six images, but they neither beautify the verse nor emphasize any particular idea. Instead they are used for comic purposes, aimed at provoking, in Rosalind and Celia, laughter and amusement. Not only is the device of accumulated images used quite functionally, but it is perfectly suited to the speaker, who is a professional jester. It is excellent fooling, though Rosalind calls him "you dull fool", perhaps because she is puzzled by the verses of Orlando which they parody, and wants to discuss the matter seriously with Celia.

Very often it so happens that a particular idea or image may not be quite apparent to the reader. There might be only a hint of an image, not a proper image at all. This is what W. Clemen has called "imagery-consciousness":

> The image which is merely suggested is a further sign of the intensive penetration of the language by the "imagery consciousness." The whole image has sunk beneath the surface, as it were, and left behind only one or two ideas connected with it.[21]

This occurs very frequently in Shakespeare. When Celia dismisses Touchstone and Corin, the former says:

> Come, shepherd, let us make an honourable retreat—though not with bag and baggage, yet with scrip and scrippage.[22]

Here we have image connected with the army, but it is only hinted at, in the phrase "honourable retreat." It is a mere suggestion, not a clear image and thus a good example of what Clemen has called "imagery consciousness."

Nearly all the images studied here have been taken from just one scene, the second scene of the fourth Act. Yet the wealth of imagery in even this one scene has not been totally explored. It can be easily imagined what a treasure-house of images the entire play might be. Intensive as well as extensive studies of Shakespeare's imagery will be very rewarding and illuminating.

REFERENCES

1. Fluchère, H., *op. cit.*, p. 167.
2. *Ibid.*
3. Act III, sc. ii, ll. 2-4, p. 41.
4. Act III, sc. ii, ll. 108-11, p. 44.
5. Act III, sc. ii, ll. 50-51, p. 42.
6. Act III, sc. ii, ll. 74-75, p. 43.
7. Act III, sc. ii, ll. 100-03, p. 44.
8. Act III, sc. ii, ll. 106-07, p. 44.
9. Act III, sc. ii, ll. 117-20, p. 44.
10. Celemen, Wolfgang, *The Development of Shakespeare's Imagery*, London, Methuen & Co. Ltd., 1977, p. 78.
11. Act III, sc. ii, ll. 155-56, p. 46.
12. Act III, sc. ii, ll. 167-71, p. 46.
13. Act III, sc. ii, ll. 198-203, p. 47.

14. Act III, sc. ii, ll. 310-29.
15. Enright, D.J. and Chickera, E. De, ed., *English Critical Texts: The Sixteenth Century to the Twentieth*, Oxford, The University Press, 2002. Dryden, An Essay on Dramatic Poesy, ll. 1498-1500, p. 88.
16. Act III, sc. ii, ll. 5-6, p. 41.
17. Act III, sc. ii, ll. 184-86, p. 46.
18. Act II, sc. v, ll. 1-4, p. 31.
19. Clemen, W., *op. cit.*, p. 81.
20. Act III, sc. ii, ll. 100-07, p. 44.
21. Clemen, W., *op. cit.*, p. 77.
22. Act III, sc. ii, ll. 161-63, p. 46.

10

Poetic Style: Diction and Versification

Style has always been an important aspect of drama, and Shakespeare's poetic style, specially, has been studied in great detail. There are several factors to be noted in this respect. His style has all the features of his age. In other words, it is an Elizabethan style. At the same time it is eloquent of his own personality. In addition, since the literary form is that of drama, different characters speak in it and the poetic style has to suit each character. The achievement, therefore, of a distinctive poetic style calls for our awestruck admiration.

Like all Elizabethan-Jacobean plays, his plays, too, were written in a mixture of prose and verse. The noble characters usually speak in verse and the humbler ones in prose. There are, however, no hard and fast rules as such. Thus in the present play both Orlando and Rosalind who are not only nobly born, but the two most important characters also, very often speak in prose.

It should be borne in mind that style has two aspects: diction and versification. These two aspects shall now be separately considered.

(A) POETIC DICTION

In ancient days the theories of classical diction were sophisticated and highly developed. These classical theories were quite well-known in the Elizabethan times, the Roman views in particular. The most famous of the classical theories of poetic diction are those of Horace who, in his *Ars Poetica* had laid down clear-cut rules of poetic diction. Apart from him there were many other writers as well, but Horace's dicta had been accepted by everyone.

According to Horace, the diction of poetry should vary according to the genre the poet was writing, but it should be modulated according to the character as well. The diction of poems dealing with sorrowful subjects, like elegies, laments, etc. should be different from that, for example, of odes or love-poems. In drama the characters should speak in a language that should suit their age, sex and social position. He makes this last point clear in a famous sentence:

> It will make a great different whether a god or a hero is speaking, a man of ripe years or a hot-headed youngster in the pride of youth, a woman of standing or an officious nurse, a roving merchant or a prosperous farmer.[1]

This sentence provides for all kinds of contingencies. First of all, divine and human characters are differentiated. This is but a simple thing. It is not so easy to differentiate between the hundreds of human characters, each with his/her own distinct profession and personality. Age must be considered as an important factor ("man of ripe years or a hot-headed youngster"), and so must sex ("woman of standing"). There is, however, a bewildering variety within these basic varieties. There are sub-divisions according to age and social status, and Horace points this out by referring to "a woman of standing or an officious nurse." He also differentiates between different professions, as for example between "a roving merchant" and a "prosperous farmer." It goes without saying that all such categories can be expanded *ad finitum*, for there are hundreds of professions. In a nutshell, the diction must suit the speaker in every way. Following these rules, diction became stringently specialized in later Elizabethan drama. Referring to this feature M.C. Bradbrook has remarked:

> The specific style for princes, for lovers, for clowns, was fixed.[2]

Certain things must always be kept in mind by the poet. The diction must be such as in natural for the speaker, it must carry out two functions as far as the reader is concerned: it must persuade the reader or the audience and it has to reach his feelings:

> The Elizabethan dramatist's style is one of impassioned poetic rhetoric, the two commonest functions of which are to persuade and to touch the emotions.[3]

In other words, the logical aspect of style as well as its affective aspect, both are equally important.

In order to achieve this double aim, the poet can, and, indeed should, make use of rhetorical devices. Aristotle, in the definition of tragedy itself, let alone later on, highlights the importance of embellishments. The style, according to the theme and the speaker, may be the grand, or the middle, or the low style, but the use of embellishments is obligatory. In Ben Jonson's *The Alchemist,* the characters belong to the lower orders and therefore when they speak the low style is used. This is about the main characters. Sir Epicure Mammon, though a minor character, belongs to the nobility and therefore when he speaks the high or the grand style is used. Both are full of figures of speech, irrespective of the speaker.

Following the classical writers, the English ones have also recommended the use of figures of speech and other rhetorical devices. George Puttenham, one of the earliest Elizabethan rhetoricians tells the poet:

> There is nothing so fitte for the poem as to be furnished with all the figures that be Rhetorical and such as do most beautific the language with eloquence.[4]

There are numerous aspects of the theories of style advanced by rhetoricians. Horace, for example, recommends the use of newly-coined words as well as the revival of words that have gone out of use. Shakespeare not only knew all the rules and concepts prevalent in his time but made continuous and effective use of them. Yet he wrote, not by rule but by instinct. There does not exist any attempt of straining or any trying for effects. Rich or simple, any style he adopts seems perfectly natural.

(i) Diction in *As You Like It*

The two decades over which Shakespeare's dramatic career stretches were years of fairly continuous development for him. All the manifold aspects of his artistry went on developing from one play to the next. His style developed as much as his art of characterization, plot-management, etc. did. *As You Like It* is a product of mature artistry and in it he has employed a diction that is eminently suited to the kind of play it is—a romantic comedy. Moreover, he adopts all the different contemporary conventions and makes them serve his own purposes. Elizabethan dramatists made use of both prose and verse and so has he. In fact he uses prose or verse not merely to indicate the social position of the characters, but also in order to heighten or lower the tone of the dialogue. Thus, even his nobly born characters use prose when talking of ordinary matters, but when a loftier or more serious tone is desired they take resort to poetry. This is a device not applicable only to the use of prose and verse but to all kinds of style, for the diction must not only suit the speaker but the situation also. In his definition of tragedy Aristotle points out that the poet must use:

> ...language enriched in a variety of ways and artistic devices appropriate to the several parts of the play.[5]

The same character, therefore, must not speak in the same manner in all the different situations in the play. Orlando, airing his grievances to Adam speaks in prose, but when he suddenly falls in love with Rosalind he cannot speak at all in her presence, and when she goes away, expresses his heightened mental state in poetry. Shakespeare modulates his style to suit the speaker as well as the situation. Even before he falls in love with Rosalind he talks to her and Celia in the second scene of the first Act. His diction there is very different indeed from how he speaks to Oliver in the first scene. This is all the more remarkable as he speaks in prose both the times and to nobly born characters. Yet there is a subtle difference in style, depending much, of course, on the delivery by the actor.

Rosalind, also, speaks in an intimate, yet light-hearted manner when she is with Celia, and in a totally different manner when rebuking Phoebe for her callousness. Oliver, when speaking to Orlando in the first scene, speaks in a most offensive blustering manner, but his diction is a totally different one when, after his change of heart, he speaks to Rosalind and Celia.

Some of the important stylistic devices used in *As You Like It* shall now be taken up. Examples will be taken from the first scene just as, in the previous chapter, examples of images had been taken from only one scene. This first scene is in prose and therefore in case there are remarkable examples in the blank verse passages elsewhere in the play, they shall be mentioned if necessary.

(ii) Stylistic Devices

There are many kinds of stylistic devices, of which, the uses of imagery, symbolism and figures of speech are the most important. Imagery has already been studied in the foregoing chapter and now some of the most important figures of speech employed by the poet shall be taken up.

Simile is a figure of speech which is the most obvious to the student. There is a simile in the first scene used by Charles when he is speaking of the banished Duke:

> ...and there they live like the old Robin Hood of England: they say many young gentlemen flock in him every day and fleet the time carelessly as they did in the golden world.[6]

Here there are two similes in one sentence. These similes here are not merely decorative ones. They beautify the diction, of course, but in addition they also anticipate the pastoral world of innocent happiness that is the typical atmosphere of this play. Likewise, in blank verse also similes occur to highlight a particular idea:

> Sweet are the uses of adversity,
> Which like the toad, ugly and venomous
> Wears yet a precious jewel in his head.[7]

Shakespeare thus can use a simile for many different purposes, whether to create the atmosphere or to point a moral, whether in prose or in poetry.

Metaphors occupy a special place among all the other figures of speech. This is because of their extraordinary effectiveness. Indeed, Greek and Roman rhetoricians give it great importance. These are to be found everywhere in the play. A humble person like Adam gives us the first metaphor in it:

> Is "old dog" my reward? Most true, I have lost my teeth in your service.[8]

This is a very simple example. The most remarkable example of metaphor in this play, of course, is the famous Seven Ages passage in which the world is compared to a stage:

> All the world's a stage,
> And all its men and women merely players;
> They have their exits and their entrances.[9]

This is a remarkable example of a metaphor which is expanded over twenty-eight lines. The world is compared with a stage and human beings to actors and then, one by one, the different stages of a man's life from infancy to senility are each described in a succession of vivid and concrete pictures or images. Such a long and colourful metaphor is indeed rare, even in a poet like Shakespeare.

Rhetorical questions impart a dramatic quality to a speech, whether in prose or in poetry. There are many passages in this play which contain a succession of rhetorical questions. Thus in the first scene there is a dialogue between Orlando and Oliver which uses four rhetorical questions in just six lines:

> Or.: Shall I keep your dogs and eat husks with them? What prodigal portion have I spent, that I should come to such penury?
>
> Ol.: Know you where you are, sir?
>
> Or.: O, sir, very well: here in your orchard.
>
> Ol.: Know you before whom, sir?[10]

In this passage the rhetorical questions have been divided between the two brothers, but there is a remarkable passage which is made entirely of rhetorical questions by one character. Rosalind has just been told that Orlando is in the forest, and she bursts out with eager curiosity:

> Alas the day, what shall I do with my doublet and hose? What did he when thou saw'st him? What said he? How looked he? Wherein went he? What makes he here? Did he ask for me? Where remains she? How parted he with thee? And when wilt thou see him again?[11]

Here we have ten rhetorical questions in very rapid succession, tumbling over each other. Nothing, in this place, would have expressed Rosalind's eager impatience as these questions do.

Shakespeare's style is well-known for its world-play. Dr. Johnson's remark in this connection has become famous:

> ...A quibble is to Shakespeare what luminous vapours are to the traveller.
>
> ...A quibble was to him the fatal Cleopatra for which he lost the world and was content to lose it.[12]

Quibbles or puns are the most obvious variety of world-play. This figure of speech is used most often by his jesters and Touchstone's speeches are full of them. But he is not the only person in the play to use pun. Thus in the first scene we have one:

> Oliver: Now, sir, what make you here?
>
> Orl.: Nothing: I am not taught to make anything.[13]

This is a very simple example of a pun, in which the word "make" is used in two senses. Later, in the speeches of Rosalind and of Touchstone we have many good and elaborate uses of pun.

Apostrophes, like rhetorical questions, add to the dramatic quality of a passage as they are directly addressed to the hearer. There are many of them in the play, though none in the first scene. The first apostrophe in the play occurs in the second scene (Act I) when Orlando, having fallen precipitately in love with Rosalind, addresses his own self in bewilderment and trepidation:

> O poor Orlando, thou art overthrown!
> Or Charles, or something weaker, masters thee.[14]

Nothing would have made the state of his mind clearer to the audience than this apostrophe. Indeed, there is hardly any other way in which it could have been expressed at all, since there is no one else in whom he could have confided or who could have wrested the secret out of him as Celia does with Rosalind.

Antithesis is not a figure of speech used frequently in poetry. The first scene, however, is in prose and Orlando uses it to great effect:

> My father charged you in his will to give me good education: you have trained me like a peasant.[15]

Though in this quarrel-scene there is but one anti-thesis, it abounds later on. In the next scene Orlando himself uses it in a far more extensive manner:

> Wherein if I be foiled, there is but one shamed that was never gracious; if killed, but one dead that is willing to be so: I shall do my friends no wrong, for I have none to lament me, the world no injury, for in it I have nothing.[16]

Often enough a sentence might have two or more figures of speech in it. Thus, Orlando tells his brother that he himself is as nobly born as Oliver is:

> ...the same tradition takes not away my blood, were there twenty brothers betwixt us.[17]

Here, first of all, "blood" symbolizes nobility, so we have an example of synecdoche, and the mention of twenty brothers is an example of hyperbole. Needless to say, such combination of two or more figures of speech makes a sentence all the more meaningful and rich.

The majority of the examples given above are taken from Orlando's speeches, and it seems that he speaks boldly and emphatically. Yet, if need arises, he can also speak indirectly, getting his effects from hints and innuendos. Thus, in the first scene he makes use of two figures based on indirectness: inversion and innuendo. The first of them sounds like a threat:

Ol.: Know you before whom, sir?

Or.: Ay, better than him I am before knows me.[18]

The highly inverted sentence by Orlando contains a hidden threat. Later he indirectly calls Oliver a villain:

> I am the youngest son of Sir Rowland de Boys, he was my father, and he is thrice a villain that says such a father begot villains.[19]

It can be seen that though in this scene Shakespeare has used prose in the middle style, yet there is no dearth of figures of speech.

Apart from figures of speech, another stylistic device employed by poets and also prose writers is the use of allusions. These can be of many types, among which mythical, literary and Biblical allusions are the most popular. Shakespeare uses all of them, though not all of them occur in the first scene. We have, however, Biblical and legendary allusions. Thus, Orlando, referring to the well-known Biblical story of the Prodigal Son asks Oliver in connection with the treatment meted out to him:

> What prodigal portion have I spent, that I should come to such penury?[20]

Here we can see the use of rhetorical question as well as a Biblical allusion, which makes this sentence all the more effective. Later when Charles comes in he uses an allusion to old legends:

> there they live like the old Robin Hood of England: they say many young gentlemen flock to him every day, and fleet the time carelessly as they did in the golden world.[21]

These two allusions to the legend of Robin Hood and to that of the Golden Age help create the pastoral atmosphere even before the audience has been taken to the forest of Arden.

One of the most famous literary allusions made by Shakespeare occurs in this play, though not in this scene. Much later in the play Phoebe the shepherdess falls headlong into love with the disguised Rosalind and quotes Marlowe's line:

Dead Shepherd, now I find thy saw of might,
"Who ever loved that loved not at first sight?"[22]

Such direct quotations are very rare in Shakespeare. Though there are many literary allusions in his plays, they usually refer to classical authors, not to his contemporaries, particularly not in such a very direct manner. We have indirect allusions, as when he parodies Kyd.

Apart from these there are many other such rhetorical devices scattered throughout the play. Only a few have been cited here and mainly from but one scene (Act I, sc. i). It can be well imagined how rich the entire play is in this respect.

(B) VERSIFICATION

As has already been pointed out, poetic style has two distinct aspects: diction and versification. The discussion of a poet's style, therefore, is but half complete without a discussion of his art of versification. This is not a purely technical part of poetry—it affects the emotional response of the reader or the audience as well. Henri Fluchère has most pertinently remarked:

> It is by its rhythm as much as by its images that a verse is expressive. The rhythmical succession has an emotional pattern, shows a purpose, imposing a mood or defining a thought.[23]

The poetic form in which Elizabethan plays were written was blank verse, though couplets were frequently used. Such a passage comprises unrhyming lines of five iambic feet. Iambic feet are disyllabic ones, of which the first is weak (or unstressed, or short) and the second is strong (or stressed or long).

Ĭ woúld / thŏu hádst / bĕen són / tŏ sóme / măn elśe,

Thĕ wórld / ĕsteḿed / thy̆ fáth / ĕr hón / oŭrab́le,

Bŭt Í / dĭd fińd / him̆ stíll / m̆ine eń/ĕmý:

Thŏu shoúld / hăve bé / ttĕr pleáśed / mĕ wíth / thĭs déed.[24]

This passage has four lines not rhyming in any way. All the feet are iambic. Each line has exactly five feet, i.e. ten syllables only, neither more, nor less. In other words, it is a passage of entirely regular blank verse. Such absolutely regular blank verse passages are difficult to find.

Blank verse has many complex features, some of which shall now be studied. One of these features is the use of end-stopped and of run-on-lines. In the passage given above the first line has a full stop at the end, i.e., the actor will have to pause there for a short time. Such a line is an end-stopped line. On the other hand, the first two lines in the passage below have no such punctuation mark at the end:

> Good Sir, I do in friendship counsel you
> To leave this place...Albeit you have deserved
> High commendation, true applause and love.[25]

Here the actor will not stop at the end of the line, but go on speaking the next without any break. Such lines are known as run-on-lines. These devices help the poet to avoid monotony in the passage. Run-on-lines give smoothness to a passage, and a succession of end-stopped lines tend to make blank verse rather jerky. A judicious mixture of both yield verse with a natural, conversational rhythm, as is desirable in drama.

Moreover, end-stopped lines need not always be avoided. An artist like Shakespeare can make use of end-stopped lines in order to enhance the naturalness and the beauty of his poetry. In an extremely moving passage, Orlando implores Duke Senior to have pity on the poor and the helpless:

> If ever you have looked on better days;
> If ever been where bells have knolled to church;
> If ever sat at any good man's feast;
> If ever from your eyelids wiped a tear,
> And know what 'tis to pity and be pitied,
> Let gentleness my strong enforcement be:
> In the which hope I blush, and hide my sword.[26]

This impassioned plea is but one long sentence (the entire sentence has not been cited here, it starts four lines earlier on) but every line has a definite pause at the end. Thus, every line gets emphasized and comes across as strongly as a hammer-blow. Had the lines been run-on ones, the catalogue would not have been so impressive.

Almost every blank verse line has a brief pause within it which is known as the caesura or the medial pause. The placing of the pause in a line is an important factor in the art of versification, for the flexibility of blank verse depends, to a large extent, on this feature. It used to be the custom in mediaeval times to place the caesura always in the middle of the line. This made the verse rather mechanical, with a jerky movement. This should be avoided in dramatic blank verse at all costs, unless of course, the writer wants to produce a special effect. The Elizabethan dramatists had to take the actor's convenience into consideration. They placed the caesura, not in the middle of the line, but at any point within the line in such a way that the actor would be easily able to draw breath and recite it. Thus, Phoebe, talking about Rosalind (who is disguised as Ganymede) speaks in a hesitating manner, stopping every now and then:

> But what care I for worlds?//—yet words do well—
> When he,// that speaks them please those that hear;
> It is a pretty youth//—not very pretty—
> But, sure, he's proud// —and yet his pride becomes him:
> He'll make a proper man:// the best thing in him
> Is his complexion;//[27]

The double vertical lines indicate the caesura. This is the positioning of the caesura in the passage:

> Line 1— after the sixth syllable
> Line 2— after the second syllable
> Line 3— after the sixth syllable
> Line 4— after the fourth syllable
> Line 5— after the sixth syllable
> Line 6— after the fifth syllable

This variations make for flexibility in the verse. Sometimes there are two, or even more, caesurae in a line. Thus, in two of the most famous lines spoken by Rosalind we have two caesurae:

> But, mistress,// know yourself//— down on your knees
> And thank heaven// fasting,// for a good man's love.[28]

Double caesurae are not very common, but they are sometimes used to emphasize certain words.

Blank verse, by definition, should have ten syllables in each line, but this rule is not a totally inflexible one. A line may often enough have more than ten syllables in it. The second of the two lines given above, for example, contains an extra syllable at the end:

> And thank/heaven/fasting/for a/good man's/love.

Just as this line has an extra syllable at the end, so may a line have less than ten syllables:

> that ever love did make thee run into,
> Thou hast not loved....[29]

The second line here has only two feet, or only four syllables in it. Silvius, speaking passionately of his love for Phoebe, breaks off in the middle of the line, too moved to go on. Such lines are highly effective and lend a natural quality to poetry.

Really good dramatic blank verse, as this brief discussion shows can never be absolutely regular iambic pentametre. There are many other metrical devices that are used to lend the desired flexibility to dramatic blank verse. One of them shall now be mentioned.

Drama is based on dialogue and very often a line is broken up between two or more speakers to avoid monotony. Known as stichomythia, this technique is often used by Shakespeare:

> Duke: Welcome... Set down your venerable burden,
> And let him feed.
>
> Orlando: I thank you most for him.
>
> Adam: So had you need.[30]

Here three different persons speak in quick succession, making up one line. Sometimes two or more persons speak individual lines, capping each other's sentence. A long conversation occurs in the play, written in a highly stylized manner:

> Silvius: It is to be all made of sighs and tears,
> And so am I for Phoebe.
>
> Ph.: And I for Ganymede.

Or.: And I for Rosalind.

Ros.: And I for no woman.[31]

Here the characters speak one line each, though the lines are each half-lines. They are, however, to be counted as full lines.

Another aspect of versification shall now be taken up—the songs. Music, according to Aristotle, is one of the six elements of drama. Elizabethan dramatists used both vocal and instrumental music in their plays and there are many songs in this play. There is, however, disagreement as to exactly how many songs there are. John Dover Wilson, for example, counts only five.[32] In other words he excludes Jaques' parody of Amiens's song in the fifth scene of the second Act, and Hymen's long marriage-song in the last scene, which comes in three parts. If we include these too, there will be seven songs, as follows:

1. Amiens's "Under the greenwood tree" (Act II, sc. v)
2. Jaques's parody of the above, "If it do come to pass" (Act II, sc. v)
3. Amiens's "Blow blow" (Act II, sc. vii)
4. Touchstone's comic song "O sweet Oliver" (Act III, sc. iii)
5. The hunting-song led by Amiens "What shall he have that killed" (Act IV, sc. ii)
6. The spring song by the Duke's two pages "It was a lover and his lass" (Act V, sc. iii)
7. Hymen's marriage-song followed by a chorus "Then there is mirth in heaven" (Act V, sc. iv).

"Under the greenwood tree" is one of the most popular songs of Shakespeare. It is the first song in the play, and carries out the function of creating the atmosphere of pastoral life. It should be always remembered that Shakespeare's songs are not there merely for purposes of entertainment, they carry out important dramatic functions also. This song is in two stanzas, consisting of a quatrain followed by a refrain of another four lines. It is a charming song which opens the fifth scene of the second Act. Amiens sings the first stanza and then is importuned by Jaques to sing the next. At first Amiens is unwilling and makes excuses but allows himself to be persuaded and sings the second stanza. An atmosphere of carefree, peaceful happy-go-lucky existence in the lap of benevolent nature is most successfully created.

Jaques's answer to the song is a parody of it, with a tone of mockery, as reply-poems often have. It is taken by many critics to mock the Duke and his followers:

> If it do come to pass,
> That any man turn ass...
> Leaving his wealth and ease,
> A stubborn will to please.[33]

This is exactly what the lords accompanying the Duke have done: they have left their homes and a life of comfort in order to follow him. Then comes the line "Ducdame, ducdame, ducdame" which he explains as "a Greek invocation to call fools into a circle"[34] but which actually is:

> a corruption of a Romany word meaning
> I foretell, or I can tell fortunes, which,
> as the call of a gipsy at fairs or public
> gatherings, is a "Greek" (=shaper's)
> invocation to call fools into a ring.[35]

Jaques's parody thus has an element of satire in it, which is not very common in Shakespeare.

"Blow blow", like "under the greenwood tree," is another anthology piece. It is a song which is sung at the request of Duke Senior in the feast scene. It is a gentle reminder that nature is not always benevolent and bountiful. The contrast with human ingratitude and hypocrisy gives this lyric a mournful tone yet the conclusion gives cause to cheer, "This life is most jolly." Both of the songs by Amiens are optimistic and give a true picture of forest life. The two complement each other, for "under the greenwood tree" tells us of spring and "Blow blow" about winter. Many critical comments are available on both.

Touchstone's comic song (Act III, sc. iii) has been counted as one of the five songs in the play by John Dover Wilson (though he does not include Jaques's parody or the long marriage-song). It is not a complete song, containing just six lines. As such, it is one of the typical stock-in-trade of a clown, who would usually sing (sometimes making them up on his own) comic songs and dance to them as Touchstone does here. As has been said earlier (*vide* the discussion on Touchstone's character in Ch. 7, *supra*) Robert Armin, an accomplished actor had joined Shakespeare's company at this time. He could sing as well as dance and his talents had inspired Shakespeare to create the great jesters of *Twelfth Night* and *King Lear*. Touchstone's song and dance foreshadows these two later and greater figures.

The hunting-song, like a drinking-song or a marriage-song is a traditional part of vocal music in a play. Here (Act IV, sc. ii) it is Jaques who calls for this song. It is a typical Elizabethan song with play on words and a long refrain. This refrain provides the chance for entertaining the audience with the element of spectacle. The man who killed the deer is dressed in deerskin and antlers and is borne aloft on the shoulders of the hunters, who form a group and march three times around a tree. John Russell Brown has compared this song with the music at Hero's tomb in *Much Ado About Nothing* and has remarked:

> One of their main justifications is that they relax the quickened pulse of action with the measure of their music and widen the focus visually with formal movement or celebration. Intellectually they are a reminder of the timeless or the general.[36]

The song sung by the two page-boys of the Duke is a song celebrating the advent of spring and of love. The play is drawing to a close, with multiple marriages in the air. The lover and his lass create the atmosphere for this ending.

Hymen's song at the end is actually part of a masque. As has been already pointed out, the masque, so popular with the Elizabethans, fulfills one of the requirements given by Aristotle—that of "opsis" or spectacle.

The masque here is a very simple one, consisting mainly of Hymen's song. It is a very colourful musical entertainment and also serves the important dramatic purpose of joining no less than four pairs of lovers in marriage. It is not such an elaborate masque as the one at the end of *The Tempest*. It opens with a song by Hymen which is interrupted after the first stanza for it is then that Rosalind talks to Duke Senior and to Orlando. Then, after this short dialogue of nine lines in which the Duke and Orlando both recognise and accept Rosalind, Hymen resumes his song. He takes each pair individually and addresses and blesses them:

> You and you no cross shall part:
> You and you are heart in heart:
> You to his love must accord
> Or have a woman to your lord.
> You and you are sure together,
> As the winter to foul weather.[37]

Thus, one after another he takes Orlando-Rosalind, Oliver-Celia, Silvius-Phoebe and Touchstone-Audrey in that order. After this there is a choric song and then the masque ends.

To sum up, once more, it is a simple masque that serves two purposes: it joins four pairs of lovers in holy matrimony in the sight of God and His representative on earth, the Duke. Secondly, it provides the element of spectacle, the last of the six elements of drama as given by Aristotle.

This long song by Hymen, which comprises two stanzas, a passage in octosyllabic couplets and a Choric song has been left out by John D. Wilson in his list of the songs in the play. Perhaps he thought that the masque is not a part of the play proper. This, strictly speaking, is not accurate, for music is very definitely one of the essentials of drama. In almost all the plays a masque occurs, usually at the end of the play.

Poetic style, in its many different aspects, is one of the facets of a play. In this chapter the figures of speech have been taken mainly from one chapter, though that is not the case with prosodic features. The earnest student will realise what enormous variety of imagery and rhetoric is scattered throughout the play. Even a limited study like the present one will make the reader realise the richness of, and the variety within, Shakespeare's poetic style.

REFERENCES

1. Dorsch, T.S., ed. & transl., *Classical Literary Criticism*, Penguin Books, 1975, p. 83.
2. Bradbrook, M.C., *op. cit.*, p. 45.
3. Fluchère, H., *op. cit.*, p. 152.
4. Quoted in *ibid.*, p. 159.
5. Dorsch, T.S., *op. cit.*, p. 39.
6. Act I, sc. i, ll. 110-13, p. 6.
7. Act II, sc. i, ll. 12-14, p. 22.
8. Act I, sc. i, ll. 78-79, p. 5.
9. Act II, sc. vii, ll. 139-41, p. 38.
10. Act I, sc. i, ll. 35-40, p. 4.
11. Act III, sc. ii, ll. 217-21, p. 47.
12. Brady, Frank and Wimsatt, W.K., ed., *Samuel Johnson: Selected Poetry and Prose*. Berkeley, University of California Press, 1975, p. 309.
13. Act I, sc. i, ll. 27-28, p. 4.
14. Act I, sc. ii, ll. 257-58, p. 16.
15. Act I, sc. i, ll. 63-64, p. 5.
16. Act I, sc. ii, ll. 176-80, p. 13.
17. Act I, sc. i, ll. 45-46, p. 4.
18. Act I, sc. i, ll. 40-41, p. 4.
19. Act I, sc. i, ll. 53-55, p. 4.
20. Act I, sc. i, ll. 36-37, p. 4.
21. Act I, sc. i, ll. 110-13, p. 6.
22. Act III, sc. v, ll. 90-91, p. 61.
23. Fluchère, H., *op. cit.*, p. 181.
24. Act I, sc. ii, ll. 211-14, pp. 14-15.
25. Act I, sc. ii, ll. 249-51, p. 16.
26. Act II, sc. vii, ll. 113-19, p. 37.
27. Act III, sc. v, ll. 111-16, pp. 62-63.
28. Act III, sc. v, ll. 57-58, p. 61.
29. Act II, sc. iv, ll. 34-35, p. 28.
30. Act II, sc. viii, ll. 67-69, p. 39.
31. Act V, sc. ii, ll. 81-84, p. 81.
32. Wilson, John Dover, *op. cit.*, p. 143.

33. Act II, sc. v, ll. 48-52, p. 32.
34. Act II, sc. v, ll. 57-58, p. 32.
35. Wilson, J.D., *op. cit.*, p. 153.
36. Brown, John Russell, *op. cit.*, p. 72.
37. Act V, sc. iv, ll. 128-33, p. 89.

11

Critical Reception: A Brief History

As You Like It has been highly popular from its very first stage-performance. It continued to be staged, with alterations, in the next few centuries and is being, at present, continually prescribed in school and college syllabi as well as taken up for serious research work. This proves its striking universal appeal for all classes of people, of all time, irrespective of the barriers imposed by religion or language or social customs.

Francis Meres does not mention it in his *Paladis Tamia* but it is well-known that on August 4, 1600, it was, together with three other plays of the Lord Chamberlaine's company, ordered to be staged. There is a tradition that Shakespeare himself used to play the role of Adam in it. There are no other records of performances till 1740. The seventeenth century, with its licentious comedy of manners, did not have much inclination for this play, but in the eighteenth century there was a revival of it in 1740 in its entirety. Before that it had provided the basis for *Love in a Forest* by Charles Johnson in 1723 who had made so many changes that it cannot be regarded as a performance of Shakespeare's play at all.

The second half of the eighteenth century onwards, however, the play has enjoyed great popularity on the stage as well as with the serious readers. Dr. Johnson made a serious though sketchy study of the play. He approves of the story ("wild and pleasing") but does not approve of "the facility with which both Rosalind and Celia give away their hearts." He praises the dialogue for its elegance and harmony. He has a very pertinent and characteristically Johnsonian remark to make about the ending:

> By hastening to the end of his work,
> Shakespeare suppressed the dialogue
> between the usurper and the hermit
> and lost an opportunity of exhibiting
> a moral lession.[1]

But a moral lesson, however edifying, would have gone against the spirit of the play (*vide* the section on Indian Dramaturgy, *infra*).

It is specially from the nineteenth century onwards that the character of Rosalind became extremely important and reviews of performances dwell specially on this character. This is the case mainly with twentieth century reviewers, but serious criticism during the nineteenth century started the trend of idolizing Rosalind. Thus, Hazlitt writes in a rapturous manner:

> Rosalind's character is made up of sportive gaiety and natural tenderness. She talks herself out of breath, only to get deeper in love... How full of laughing grace is all her conversation with Orlando.... How full of real fondness and pretended cruelty is her answer to him when he promises to love her "For ever and a day!"[2]

There had been faithfully realistic productions in the beginning of the twentieth century and then the fashion for experiments set in. There was an all-male production in 1967 with psychedelic settings and costumes:

> The trees of Arden become glass tubes and plastic roofings in punched out patterns, like computer tapes. The clothes are pastel uniforms, tricked out with gold and silver PVC capes and boots. Visually, it is a cross between a Pierre Cardin shop-window and "The Shape of things to Come."[3]

In 1973, there was a production in modern dress and a musical in 1977. Such experimental stagings have continued and, will, doubtless, also continue in future, for it is one of the most stage-worthy plays of Shakespeare, versatile enough to lend itself to different interpretations.

As far as literary criticism is concerned, this is one of those plays which have never suffered any eclipse in its popularity. The critics of the eighteenth and the nineteenth centuries noticed the strong character-delineation, the intricacies of the plot, and the beauty of the set speeches. David Erskine Baker, in 1764, pointed out that it is equally effective on the stage and as closet-reading. Dr. Johnson whose views have already been quoted above-mentioned, though briefly, all the features of the play in a sentence each and had but one fault to find, and that is with the ending.

The most important critical opinion of early nineteenth century is that of Hazlitt who, in the typical manner of Romantic critics, lays stress upon the affective aspect of the play:

> Caprice and fancy reign and revel here, and stern necessity is banished to the court. The mild sentiments of humanity are strengthened with thought and leisure.[4]

Dowden relates the play to the life of the writer and points out that it provides a respite to Shakespeare from the labours of writing serious plays:

> Shakespeare turns with a sense of relief and a long easeful sigh, from the oppressive subject of history, so grave, so real, so massive, and finds rest and freedom and pleasure in escapes from courts and camps to the forest of Arden.[5]

In the twentieth century different schools of criticism came rapidly into existence and the scholars eagerly turned to Shakespeare as to a true touchstone, trying out their theories. All the different features of his plays—the theme, the plot, the characters, etc. were also taken up and studied in detail. Thus, Caroline Spurgeon and Wolfgang Clemen studied the imagery in his plays in two well-known books (cited in the relevant chapters). H.B. Charlton's work estimated how much Shakespeare was indebted to his classical and English predecessors, though, of course, his work is no pedantic assessment of the influences on Shakespeare—it is a very illuminating study of some of the comedies. M.C. Bradbrook has given a study of the contemporary dramatic social and stage conventions. Both of these critics have been extensively referred in the preceding pages. A faithful research into the sources of his plays was made by Geoffrey Bullough, the second volume of whose monumental *Narrative and Dramatic Sources of Shakespeare* contains the sources of *As You Like It* (*vide* Ch. 8, *supra*). Studies relating the play to contemporary society as well as to the many philosophical concepts of the time have shed new lights on it. L.A. Montrose, for example, looks at the legal and social conventions of primogeniture that gave everything to the eldest son and deprived the younger ones. He analyses the play as illustrating this theme from the viewpoint of Orlando as the youngest son who leads a neglected existence and emerges triumphant in the end. Feminist criticism looks at the social and economic position of women in Elizabethan times and analyses the play as well as the characters from this point of view.

Studies of his plays from the point of view of Indian poetics have not been so frequent. A very sketchy account of this play from the point of view of Indian poetics is given below.

Indian Dramaturgy

The Indian theory of drama goes back to the *Nāṭyaśāstra* of the sage Bharata. By the time that Ācārya Dhananjaya wrote his famous *Daśarūpaka* ten kinds of plays (*rūpakas*) had come to be generally accepted. This classification was made keeping three elements in mind, that is, the content, the characters and the *aṅgī rasa*:

Vastu, netā, rasāsṭeṣāṅ bhedako vastu ca tridhā.[6]

That is to say, the subject-matter, the hero and the *rasa*, the differences in these three give rise to the differences among the *rūpakas* or plays.

As You like It, according to this and other detailed specifications given later, would be a *nāṭikā*. According to the rules, the story in a *nāṭikā* should be a *prakhyāta* or well-known one, like those in the scriptures, etc. The story with which our play deals, though well-known, does yet not have the status of a classical or a Biblical one. It is neither *prakhyāta* (well-known), nor is it an *utpādya* one, for it is not entirely the dramatist's own creation. *Utpādya* (imaginary) stories can be used in a *nāṭikā*, or *saṅkara* (mixed) ones, and our story comes within this last category.

Likewise the hero Orlando is not a *prakhyāta* character like one from the epics (Troilus in *Troilus and Cressida*) or a historical figure (like Henry V and others). He, too, is *utpādya*, or, rather, *saṅkara*.

The main *rasa* or the *aṅgī rasa* of such a play should be *śṛṅgāra* or the Erotic *rasa*. *As You Like It*, being a romantic comedy, has love as its main theme (*vide* Ch. 7, *supra*). This *rasa*, moreover is in keeping with the three conditions necessary for the *aṅgīrasa*. The first of these is *vahuvyāpti*, i.e., that it should be the *rasa* which is the one most frequently evoked in the play, the second is that it should motivate the main characters and the third is *phalāgama*, i.e., the aim and end of the play should be in keeping with the *rasa*. In the present case, all three are fulfilled. When analysed in detail it would be found that *śṛṅgāra* is the most frequently evoked *rasa* in the play, that the main characters are motivated by it and at the end there are four marriages. Marriage or union of lovers is definitely the desired end of *śṛṅgāra rasa*.

The main plot of a play is known as the *adhikārika* and related actions as *prāsaṅgika*. In our play we have both. Thus, the main plot is that of Rosalind and Orlando, and the others are all *prāsaṅgika*. These, in turn are divided into two kinds, *patākā* and *prakarī*. The plot concerning the Duke and his followers can be called a *patākā*:

Sānubandhaṅ patākākhyaṅ prakarī ca pradeśabhāk.[7]

A *patākā*, in other words, continues till the end of the play whereas a *prakarī* does not. Duke Senior's plot is therefore a *patākā* and the others are but *prakarīs*. It may be said that the other sub-plots also carry on to the end, but they do not begin early in the play. The Silvius-Phoebe, Touchstone-Audrey and Oliver-Celia plots all come quite late in the play. These *prakarīs* are similar to the main plot in that the dominant *rasa* in them is *śṛṅgāra* and thus they not only support the main plot but also help fulfill the conditions necessary for a *rasa* to be the *aṅgī rasa* of a play.

The arrangement of the incidents or the progress of the plot has been divided into several stages. A detailed analysis of the play, which is not possible here, will make these stages clear, for they too, exist in our play. Almost every stage given in Sanskrit dramaturgy can be parallelled here. Orlando's decision to compete in the wrestling-match, for example, is the *bīja*.

As far as the characters go, Orlando the hero is, as indeed the hero of a *nāṭikā* should be, a truly perfect example of a *dhīra-lalita* hero. *Ācārya* Dhananjaya has defined such a hero thus:

Niścinto dhīra-lalitah kalāsaktah sukhī mṛduh.[8]

In other words, the *dhīra-lalita* hero is of a carefree nature, loves the arts, is comfort-loving and gentle in manners. There are two romantic heroes in Shakespeare who fulfill all these requirements: Orsino of *Twelfth Night* and Orlando. Duke Orsino loves music but he himself does not write poetry. Orlando does one better in that he himself writes poetry. Again, the *dhira-lalita* hero is of a carefree disposition (*niścinto*) and once Orlando reaches the forest this aspect of his character comes to the fore. Moreover, it is then that Orlando the lover fully expresses himself and the only cares or worries he has at this stage are the ones of love—not only admissible but expected in a romantic lover.

Both Oliver and Frederick are *prati-nāyakas*. Such characters are defined thus:

Lubdho dhīroddhatah stabdhah pāpakṛduyasanī ripuh.[9]

That is, he is greedy, *dhīroddhata*, quiet, sinful, sensual and the hero's enemy. Most of these epithets fit both of these characters except that of being sensual. To take them one by one, the fact that Oliver lifts his hand against his own brother bears out the quick temper of a *dhīroddhata* hero. The quick anger of Frederick against Orlando and later against Rosalind that makes him spurn the former and banish the latter does the same for him. Both of them are without doubt greedy and sinful for Oliver not only decides to deprive Orlando of the thousand crowns that are his due but plots his death. Frederick, greedy for power, usurps the kingdom of his elder brother and confiscates the lands of his followers as well as those of Oliver. A detailed study will make these correspondences clearer.

Coming to the heroine, there are many kinds of them in Sanskrit dramaturgy, with their various and manifold attributes. Shakespeare's heroines, for the most part, defy all labels and attempts at any kind of classification, but Rosalind can be said to fall within the category of *madhya-adhīrā nāyikā*. Such a heroine chides her beloved with laughter and irony as Rosalind does again and again:

> Why, how now, Orlando! Where have you been all this while? You a lover! An you serve me such another trick, never come in my sight more.[10]

When during the love-game Rosalind pretends to reject him, Orlando says he would die. Rosalind then counters by ridiculing such protestations and says:

> Men have died from time to time, and worms have eaten them, but not for love.[11]

Three of the heroines of these four golden comedies are of this type: Portia (*The Merchant of Venice*), Beatrice (*Much Ado About Nothing*), and Rosalind. Viola of *Twelfth Night* is different, for she is quiet and self-effacing.

A detailed analysis of this, or indeed, any other play of Shakespeare from the point of view of Indian poetics will cast revealing light on the play. One such point may be mentioned here. Earlier in this chapter Dr. Johnson's views, in which he disapproves of the ending of the play, had been cited. From the viewpoint of Indian poetics it may be said that a dialogue between Frederick and the hermit at the end would have evoked *śānta rasa*, which would have gone against the *aṅgī rasa* of the play. Shakespeare's inborn aesthetic sense must have rebelled against something that went so clearly against the spirit of the play and that is why there is no such scene in the play.

REFERENCES

1. Brown, John Russell, *op. cit.*, p. 28.
2. *Ibid.*, p. 34.
3. *Ibid.*, p. 240.
4. *Ibid.*, p. 33.
5. *Ibid.*, p. 36.
6. Dwivedi, Hazari Prasad and Dwivedi, Prithvinatha, *Nāṭyaśāstra kī Paramparā aur Daśarūpaka*, New Delhi, Rajkamal Prakashan, 1971, p. 67.
7. *Ibid.*, p. 68.
8. *Ibid.*, p. 113.
9. *Ibid.*, p. 122.
10. Act IV, sc. i, ll. 37-39, p. 65.
11. Act IV, sc. i, ll. 101-03, p. 66.

12

Important Questions

1. "What gives Shakespeare's romantic comedies their uniqueness is the nature of the specific conflict which for a time frustrates their love stories." Do you agree? Illustrate your answer with references to *As You Like It*.
2. "The conflict between the pastoral convention and reality includes the motif of pastoral love and its literary conventions." Elucidate, with special reference to *As You Like It*.
3. "Shakespeare's concern (in *As You Like It*) is not for the pastoral theme itself but for what it can be made to express." Do you agree? Give reasons for your answer.
4. "In Touchstone Shakespeare presents the ironic satirist of both idealized pastoralism and realistic love." Analyse the character of Touchstone in the light of this remark.
5. "Jaques's attitude towards the pastoral is not directly satirical." Do you agree?
6. "Jaques's view of the human condition is extreme and for that reason unacceptable." Elucidate.
7. "The Duke's pastoralism is coloured by a sentimentality and conscious melancholy." Give your own comments.
8. "Rosalind remains a romantic lover to the end, even though she seems to mock every association with romantic love." Elucidate.
9. "Rosalind is made to affect and control not only changes in a character's attitude but also the movement and direction of the play's action." Elucidate.

10. "Rosalind is no symbolic character. She is far too human for that." Comment with reference to the text.
11. "*As You Like It* is also a sentimentalist." Elucidate with illustrations.
12. "*As You Like It* is pattern play and demands brains in the true performing of it." Elucidate.
13. "In the shimmering air of Romance which the inhabitants of Arden breathe, love is the main industry." How far is this true of *As You Like It*?
14. "Shakespeare's images adopt themselves more and more organically to the structural form of the drama." Explain with special reference to *As You Like It*.
15. Write a note on Shakespeare's poetic style with special reference to *As You Like It*.

Bibliography

Bradbrook, M.C., *The Growth and Structure of Elizabethan Comedy*, London, Chatto and Windus, 1955.

——, *Elizabethan Stage Conditions*, Cambridge, The University Press, 1968.

Brown, J.R., *Shakespeare and His Comedies*, London, Methuen, 1957.

——, Shakespeare; *Much Ado About Nothing and As You Like It: A Casebook*, London, Macmillan, 9th Reprint, 1992.

Bullough, G., *The Narrative and Dramatic Sources of Shakespeare*, London, Routledge & Kegan Paul, Vol. II, 1958.

Champion, L.S., *The Evolution of Shakespeare's Comedies,* Harvard, University Press, 1973.

Charlton, H.B., *Shakespeare's Comedies*, London, Methuen, 1977.

Clemen, W., *The Development of Shakespeare's Imagery*, London, Methuen, 1977.

Ribner, Irving, *William Shakespeare: Life, Times and Theatre*, New Delhi, Wiley Easter Ltd., 1978.

Senjufla, S.C., *Shakespearean Comedy*, London, OUP, 1950.

Tillyard, E.M.W., *The Elizabethan World Picture*, New York, Vintage Books, no date.

Wilson, John Dover, *Shakespeare's Happy Comedies,* London, Faber & Faber, no date.

Index